HONEST TO GOODNESS

HONEST TO GOODNESS

Everyday RECIPES *for the* HOME COOK

CHRISTINE **TIZZARD**

whitecap

EDITORS Jordie Yow and Patrick Geraghty
DESIGN Andrew Bagatella
FOOD PHOTOGRAPHY Reena Newman
FOOD STYLING Christine Tizzard and Reena Newman
PROOFREADER Patrick Geraghty

Printed in Canada

Library and Archives Canada Cataloguing in Publication
Tizzard, Christine, 1976-, author
Honest to goodness / Christine Tizzard.
ISBN 978-1-77050-302-1 (softcover)
1. Cooking. 2. Cookbooks. I. Title.
TX714.T59 2017 641.5 C2017-900784-X

We acknowledge the financial support of the Government of Canada through the Canada Book Fund (CBF) for our publishing activities and the Province of British Columbia through the Book Publishing Tax Credit.

Nous reconnaissons l'appui financier du gouvernement du Canada et la province de la Colombie-Britannique par le Book Publishing Tax Credit.

Canada

17 18 19 20 21 22 6 5 4 3 2 1

To my family.

STAUB

CONTENTS

INTRODUCTION

MY STORY

Cooking is my escape. Being both nostalgic and challenging, it helps to clear my mind, leaving me with that simple feeling of peace. I like to think that my approach to food is easygoing, loving and respectful. Feeding my family, however, has been a bit more of a challenge.

Like anyone, I am constantly striving for a sense of balance in my life—I want to be a good mother, I want to work hard, I want to make everyone happy and I want to find happiness for myself along the way. I find pleasure in cooking, so cooking for my family at home makes sense to me. But even for someone like me who works with food every day as a chef, recipe developer and food stylist, I still struggle to put stress-free healthy meals on the table. Especially ones that the whole family will actually eat!

I first learned about cooking from watching my parents. My dad cooked most of our dinners, my mom baked up a storm and both took pleasure in the process. That was the first and most important food lesson I learned. My career in food started when I decided to go to chef school, despite not knowing where I would end up in the industry. Food was the only thing that really interested me, and it was a passion I needed to follow. My previous background in TV and film as an actor made the world of food TV very appealing, both behind the scenes as a food stylist and culinary consultant, as well as in front of the camera as a cooking show host and food educator. It gave me a way to connect in a real way with real people.

This cookbook is my way of telling you that you are not alone. I know sitting down to share a family meal together is far from easy. I wrote this cookbook because I want to help make your journey with food a little bit easier. I understand all too well how little control we have over our lives, but one thing I do have control over is what I put on the table. Setting the table is my way of setting a good example. This has helped me find peace.

WHY I WROTE THIS COOKBOOK

I love teaching people about food. Isn't that what a cookbook is supposed to do? Inspire and educate with the added bonus of pretty pictures? The most gratifying thing people say to me is that I make cooking look easy, so I wrote a book providing you with easy-to-follow recipes that leave you feeling more confident in your kitchen. I also wanted to share with you all the little things I have learned about food that have simplified my life when cooking at home.

The biggest struggle I have cooking at home is my ongoing attempt to make everyone happy with what we are having for dinner. On top of keeping my kids satisfied, I struggle with feeding the never-ending flow of children in and out of my house, topped with my insatiable love of dinner parties. I love food, and—I know—I do it to myself! So I have written a cookbook that helps with all of the ever-changing menus and often shortened prep times.

This "from scratch" cookbook is inspired by the love and passion I have for food and family meals. When I say "from scratch" I mean actually preparing meals from the ground up, starting with the base raw ingredients. I believe this is the best way to build a healthy cooking foundation. It doesn't mean I don't use prepared foods when I need to, like a favourite tomato sauce or dressing, just that I prefer, and would like to teach you how, to make these things at home.

Most the time when we cook at home it feels like a chore, but food should be fun. I see more and more people getting absorbed in food trends and niche diets and struggling to keep up. But trends don't last, and I want to instill a positive and encouraging approach to food—all people need are practical, easy and accessible recipes made with humble, nutrient-dense ingredients. I want you to be able to sit down and eat, whether it's by yourself, or around a table full of kids and chatter. This is where memories are made!

With all of these different mouths to feed, I am extremely sympathetic to dietary restrictions and food allergies. The guilt of having a child's mouth swell because someone sliced watermelon on the same cutting board that someone made a peanut butter sandwich on is nothing I would wish on anyone. Been there, done that. With the increasing number of food allergies and sensitivities, I wanted to feature gluten-free, vegetarian, vegan and healthy nut-free alternatives, which is a great aspect of this cookbook, even if your family is allergy-free. Maybe because of the constant stream of dinners at my house, I also have a love affair with leftovers, so many of the recipes in this book will inspire you to use them up.

I like to think that I combine real food with real life, so I have strived to make each chapter straightforward and educational without being overwhelming. Being a single mother of two, it was essential to include chapters dedicated to those dreaded school lunches and last minute bake sales. There are lots of cookbooks out there and more and more being published daily telling you how you should eat. Being a chef, I have a responsibility to keep myself up to speed with food politics, fads and diets—weeding in and out and saving bits and pieces along the way. This cookbook is my honest attempt to share all the valuable information I have learned over the years, as both a chef and mother.

Ultimately, this book was aimed to employ my quality-over-quantity real-food motto. Why not get the most out of your meals? In the long run, it is your family that will feel better for it.

I love my family. I love to cook. Cook with love and love to cook.

Christine

THE ANATOMY OF A RECIPE

Before you start a recipe, read it through. Make sure you have all the ingredients and equipment on hand to make the recipe in the suggested time.

Recipes are labelled as vegan [V], gluten-free [GF], low sugar [LS] and nut-free [NF]. Low sugar refers to recipes that have been tested with low amounts (or no) natural sweeteners like honey or maple syrup.

Each recipe will project servings, based on realistic serving sizes (or what I believe an average adult would eat at home).

(NF, LS)

CAULIFLOWER MAC AND CHEESE WITH PROSCIUTTO

This is my lightened up version of a comfort food classic—and an obvious favourite around the dinner table at my house. Think mac and cheese meets cauliflower with cheese sauce. The best part is that there is a whole head of cauliflower in this recipe, so you're getting a good serving of vegetables with every bite.

The "Special Equipment Needed" section will inform you of specific tools you may need to execute the recipe above and beyond basic household kitchen items.

MAKES 6–8 servings
PREP TIME 40 minutes
COOK TIME 20 minutes
SPECIAL EQUIPMENT NEEDED casserole dish (9 × 9 inches/23 × 23 cm) or a large cast-iron pan, blender or food processor

Recipes were timed with all ingredients gathered in front of me. Times included are prep and cook, which makes it easier to divide up your day. When it comes to cook times, please note that ovens, barbecues, pots and pans all differ. I do provide guidelines on what to look for when something is "done."

- ¼ lb (125 g) sliced prosciutto, roughly chopped
- 2 cups (500 mL) brown rice macaroni
- 1 large head of cauliflower, cut into large florets
- 1 cup (250 mL) chicken stock
- 3 Tbsp (45 mL) butter, plus extra for greasing casserole dish
- ½ onion, grated
- 2 cloves garlic, puréed
- 3 Tbsp (45 mL) all-purpose flour
- 1½ cups (375 mL) whole milk
- 1 Tbsp (15 mL) Dijon mustard
- ½ tsp (2 mL) cayenne
- 1 tsp (5 mL) smoked paprika
- Freshly grated nutmeg to taste
- 1 cup (250 mL) grated medium cheddar cheese
- 1 cup (250 mL) grated Gruyère cheese
- Salt to taste
- Pepper to taste
- ¾ cup (185 mL) grape tomatoes, cut in half
- ⅓ cup (80 mL) (approx.) grated Parmesan for topping
- "All Dressed" Kale Chips, for garnish (see p. xx; optional)

1. Preheat oven to 400°F (200°C) and grease casserole dish or cast-iron frying pan with butter.
2. Preheat sauté pan over medium-high heat. Add chopped prosciutto and cook until crispy, about 2–3 minutes. Set aside in bowl.
3. Boil pasta in boiling salted water, according to package directions; drain and set aside.
4. Steam cauliflower florets over boiling salted water in a double boiler (or steamer insert) until fork tender. Transfer half of the steamed cauliflower into a blender or food processor and purée with stock until smooth. Chop remaining cauliflower florets into smaller florets.
5. In a large saucepot, over medium-low heat melt butter until foamy. Add onion and garlic, and cook 3–5 minutes until softened.
6. Stir in flour and continue to cook, while stirring, for 3 minutes.
7. Slowly whisk in milk to prevent lumps from forming, then whisk in cauliflower purée and continue to simmer sauce over medium heat, stirring occasionally¬ until thickened, about 3-5 minutes.
8. Whisk in Dijon, cayenne, smoked paprika and nutmeg. Add grated cheddar and Gruyère cheese and keep on low heat until melted. Season with salt and pepper.
9. Fold cooked pasta, chopped cauliflower and prosciutto into cheese sauce. Spoon into a greased dish.
10. Sprinkle over Parmesan and scatter halved grape tomatoes on top. Bake approximately 20 minutes or until bubbling and browned on top.

When instructions call for you to "preheat" a pan or pot, it means that you should heat the pan first over the suggested heat source until hot, then add your oil, then the ingredients. One very common mistake I see people making in the kitchen is adding food to a cold or slightly warm pan. This causes your food to stick or boil instead of searing, and creates uneven and/or longer cooking times.

"Greasing" or "lining" a baking sheet means use whatever you have on hand. Oil, butter, parchment or a silicon baking mat. If I say to use something in particular there is a reason why, usually for flavour.

When baking, use the centre rack if not otherwise noted.

NOTES ABOUT THE INGREDIENTS

- Butter is always unsalted to better control salt intake and flavour in recipes, especially when baking.
- Eggs are always large.
- Salt is always kosher or coarse, unless otherwise specified. These salts have slightly larger grains than table salt. I can feel them in my fingers, which makes for a more even distribution when seasoning and also prevents over-salting. Get rid of that salt shaker and get used to pinching salt out of a bowl.
- Pepper is always freshly ground from a pepper mill for freshest flavour.
- Feel, taste and smell your food as it is cooking. Seasoning along the way, instead of at the very end, will help develop better flavours.
- It is assumed that you are washing your fruits and vegetables.
- Buying seasonal local produce will end up being the most budget friendly. I buy organic only when affordable.
- When referring to any stock or broth I use home-made, low or no salt added.
- "Neutral-tasting oil" means any oil that has a neutral flavour and a higher smoke point, like avocado, canola, sunflower, rice bran or grapeseed oil.
- "Milk of choice" means cow, nut, rice, seed, coconut or lactose-free. Whatever your family likes to use.
- "All-purpose flour of choice" means regular, organic or gluten-free.

THE BASICS

Sometimes the only way to guarantee you are eating real food made from natural ingredients is by making it from scratch. Starting with these basic recipes, we can learn to build a foundation of flavours that are always within arm's reach.

These basic homemade recipes also double as ingredients in other recipes in this cookbook, so making them gives you the necessary tools to cook from scratch.

(GF, NF, LS)

JUST YOGURT

One of my first eureka food moments was stumbling upon a recipe for yogurt in a culinary textbook the week before culinary school started. The simple two-ingredient recipe changed my approach to food. I thought, "of course!" when I read it. Of course I can make my own yogurt. All I need is milk and yogurt. It couldn't be any more basic.

Discovering this recipe was perfect timing as I had started feeling overwhelmed and frustrated checking out the yogurt aisle. Reading through the listed ingredients, I found flavoured yogurts too sweet and some of the ingredients questionable. Almost all of them contained some sort of "natural flavour," or unnecessary ingredients. I'd had enough. I made my own.

MAKES 4 cups (1 L)
PREP TIME 15 minutes
INCUBATION TIME 7–12 hours
SPECIAL EQUIPMENT NEEDED heavy-bottomed saucepot or Dutch oven with lid, digital thermometer, 4-cup (1 L) sterilized jar with lid, heating pad (optional)

4 cups (1 L) whole milk

¼ cup (60 mL) plain yogurt, reserved from previous batch or store bought (see Yogurt Tips below)

1. Heat milk in a heavy-bottomed saucepot over medium heat until scalding (just before first boil), and the temperature on a digital thermometer shows 185°F (85°C).
2. Remove from heat and let cool until just warm to the touch and temperature reads 110°F (43°C), about 10–15 minutes.
3. Once cooled, whisk in yogurt, cover with a lid and place in a warm spot (the inside of an oven with the light left on, on top of a heating pad, or even wrapped in tea towels) for several hours or overnight. The residual heat from the pot helps with the incubation time. Note: fluctuations in kitchen temperatures can influence fermentation time.
4. Once thickened, stir and store in a clean glass jar in the fridge for up to 2 weeks, making sure to reserve ¼ cup (60 mL) of this homemade yogurt for the next batch. Making yogurt at home, you will notice that it may not be as thick as store bought and also milder in flavour at first. The flavour will develop with each batch you make.

SAVED MY LIFE: A DIGITAL THERMOMETER

The first time I bought a digital thermometer was for culinary school and now I can't believe I survived all those years without one. To think of how many times I sliced into a piece of meat to see if it was cooked, letting all the flavourful juices flow out! If there is one thing you should invest in, besides a good knife, it is a good digital thermometer. You will thank me for it.

YOGURT TIPS

- When buying store-bought yogurt for your first batch, choose a plain yogurt with many types of bacterial cultures listed in its ingredients. The more variety of cultures the better.
- Yes, you can make yogurt using low-fat milk. However, the more fat, the thicker and creamier the yogurt.
- I have accidentally forgotten that I have milk cooling, and yes, added the yogurt to the milk after it has fallen below 100°F (40°C). Oops. All this may do is prolong the incubation time.
- Want Greek yogurt? Drain yogurt in a cheesecloth-lined strainer fit over a bowl overnight in your fridge. This strains off its liquid whey. You can use this whey to make my Cheap and Simple Sauerkraut (see p. 28).

(V, GF, NF, LS)

HOMEMADE MUSTARD

Yes, I make my own mustard. Not to say I don't have a good bottle of Dijon in my fridge, but making your own is a wonderful way to liven up a fridge door, plus your dinner guests will be super impressed. You can make this simple recipe as a cool little kitchen experiment for kids, and I have also been known to hand out small mason jars of our homemade mustard to friends and family as holiday gifts. Yep, that's me.

MAKES about ¾ cup (185 mL)
PREP TIME 5 minutes
STAND TIME 3 days
SPECIAL EQUIPMENT NEEDED food processor or blender

- ⅓ cup (80 mL) yellow mustard seeds
- ⅓ cup (80 mL) white wine vinegar
- ⅓ cup (80 mL) white wine of your choice
- 3 Tbsp (45 mL) maple syrup or honey
- 1 tsp (5 mL) ground turmeric
- ½ tsp (2 mL) salt
- ¼ tsp (1 mL) cayenne
- 2–3 Tbsp (30–45 mL) water (optional)

1. In a covered glass bowl or mason jar, stir together all ingredients except water. Let stand at room temperature for 3 days. Mustard seeds will swell and soften, absorbing all the flavours. At this point, you can use it as-is for a grainy mustard or, for smoother mustard, process in a food processor or blender until coarsely textured, adding 2–3 Tbsp (30–45 mL) water to loosen mixture if too thick.
2. Transfer to clean glass jars with lids and keep refrigerated. Mustard keeps for up to 6 months so make sure to label and date your jar.

MUSTARD TIPS

- There are three main varieties of mustard seed. Yellow (sometimes called white) is the easiest to find and has a milder, nuttier flavour, while brown and black seeds have more heat. Try a mixture of brown and yellow mustard seeds, keeping in mind the brown seeds pack more intensity.
- Want to step it up a notch? Add other flavour notes with fresh herbs like thyme, tarragon or rosemary. To do this, bring wine and vinegar to a boil, remove from heat, add a few sprigs of fresh herbs and cover. Let herbs steep as you would tea. Once cool, strain out herbs and proceed with the recipe.
- Mustard is not just a condiment. Try adding a tablespoon to your next sauce, vinaigrette or marinade for an instant flavour boost.

(V, GF, NF, LS)

CANNED TOMATOES IN JARS

Setting aside one weekend at the end of summer with my good friend, a bushel (or two) of tomatoes and a few bottles of wine has become a tradition. There is a lot of girl talk while tackling enough of these canned tomatoes to last us both through the winter. It makes whipping up a sauce, salsa, bruschetta topping, stew or soup a breeze, all year long.

Of course, it wouldn't be a tradition if one of us didn't mention how it's called canning but doesn't use cans—canning is done with jars.

This is a very small-batch recipe, perfect for newbies. I suggest doubling or tripling it once you fall in love with these tomatoes. If you're going to start up that boiling-water canner, you might as well make a day of it!

Note: use the freshest, ripest produce you can find. Be clean and sterilize your jars properly. Ring bands can be reused but always use new lids and use undamaged standard canning jars.

MAKES enough for four 2-cup (500 mL) jars
PREP TIME 1 hour
CANNING TIME 40 minutes
SPECIAL EQUIPMENT NEEDED boiling-water canner, four 2-cup (500 mL) mason jars with lids and ring bands, boiling-water canning kit (optional), slotted spoon or spider spoon

2 kg (4.5 lb) basket Roma tomatoes

16 fresh basil leaves

1 tsp (5 mL) citric acid or ¼ cup (60 mL) bottled or fresh lemon juice (see Canning Tomato Tips below)

4 garlic cloves, peeled

2 fresh chili peppers, cut in half lengthwise (optional)

1. Prepare a boiling-water canner by filling it with water. Sterilize jars by placing them in the canner while the water is being brought to a boil; once boiling, leave jars for 10 minutes. (Alternatively, run clean jars through a hot cycle in your dishwasher with no soap.) Set the ring bands aside, no sterilization needed. Heat the new lids in a small pot of hot water, but do not boil. Jars and lids should be kept warm until ready to use.
2. Fill a large saucepot with water and bring to a boil. Slice an "X" at the bottom end of each tomato and remove stems with a paring knife. Blanch tomatoes by plunging them in boiling water for 2 minutes, then transferring with a slotted spoon or spider spoon (see Saved My Life below) to a large bowl or clean sink filled with ice-cold water. Blanching stops the cooking process and makes the tomatoes easier to peel. With the help of a paring knife, remove skins. They should slip off easily.
3. This part is messy. Cut tomatoes into quarters, removing seeds as you go. Do this over a bowl fit with a mesh sieve, reserving tomato juice. Place quartered tomatoes in another large bowl and toss with basil leaves.
4. Put ¼ tsp (1 mL) citric acid or 1 Tbsp (15 mL) lemon juice, 1 garlic clove and half a chili pepper into each jar. Using a canning funnel or small ladle, start filling up jars with chopped tomatoes, pressing down as you go with clean fingers or the back of a wooden spoon. This helps release trapped air bubbles. Pour in reserved tomato juice, leaving ½ inch (1 cm) of headroom.

5. Wipe rims of jars clean with a damp paper towel and, using a magnetic canning lifter (or tongs), place one warm lid on top of each jar. Screw ring bands on until they are what is known in the canning world as "three-fingertip tight" (use three fingertips to screw bands on until resistance is met). This way water can't get in but air can be released, creating a proper seal.
6. Using canning tongs (or regular tongs), carefully place jars in the canner so boiling water covers the tops of the jars by at least 1 inch (2.5 cm). Cover and leave jars in the boiling water for 40 minutes.
7. Remove lid, turn off heat and let jars sit in hot water for 5 minutes before carefully lifting jars out with tongs. Place jars on a tea towel–lined surface or cooling rack. Do not disturb for 24 hours.
8. Check seals by seeing if the lids pop up and down when you press on them. If they pop up and down, they failed to seal and you should refrigerate and use within the next few days. Store sealed jars in a cool dark place.

SAVED MY LIFE: MY SPIDER SPOON

This inexpensive skimmer, used in Asian cooking, has a spoon-like wire mesh basket attached to a long bamboo handle. Use it like a small colander for gathering food like these tomatoes out of hot liquid. This is the best tool for simmering things with different cook times in the same pot.

CANNING TOMATO TIPS

- Roma tomatoes have the best size and texture for canning. However, preserve any variety of tomato you wish.
- You can also can skin-on whole tomatoes, but I like to take the extra time to peel and chop them to avoid this task down the road. I thank myself in the middle of winter when I grab a jar for a quick salsa or sauce. I also am picky about skins and seeds in my sauces.
- Why the citric acid or lemon juice? Boiling-water canning is best for high-acid foods, like apples and berries. Tomatoes are a medium-acid fruit with varying PH levels, so we do this to increase the acidity and ensure food safety. You can find citric acid in the baking or preserving sections of most large chain grocers.
- The only issue I have had over the years when canning and preserving is with jar breakage. This is rare and occurs due to unforeseeable hairline scratches in very old jars. It sucks. So when using older jars, I do suggest letting one jar hit the boiling water for a few minutes before adding the rest. Just in case.

(V, GF, NF, LS)

PURE VANILLA EXTRACT

Vanilla is a very common flavour enhancer. To make pure vanilla extract you have to capture the essence of real vanilla beans in alcohol. Almost any prepackaged sweet or baked good you purchase will have vanilla listed somewhere on the label, but are they using the real thing? Rarely do you see "pure vanilla extract" used. You do, however, see "natural vanilla flavour," "vanilla syrup" or "vanilla essence" listed.

If you do any amount of baking at home, I strongly suggest you get started on a batch of vanilla extract—you will wonder why you didn't do it sooner. It is one of the easiest things to make and it will end up saving you money in the long run.

MAKES ½ cup (125 mL)
PREP TIME 5 minutes
INFUSION TIME 2 weeks
SPECIAL EQUIPMENT NEEDED clean recycled bottle or jar with tight fitting lid (a dark bottle is better for avoiding sun exposure), funnel (optional)

- 8 vanilla beans, cut in half then lengthwise, exposing seeds
- 1 cup (250 mL) vodka of choice

1. Add vanilla beans and vodka to a clean bottle or jar, using a funnel if necessary. Close lid.
2. Store in a cool dark place and shake daily for 2 weeks.
3. Use as needed. You can recycle vanilla pods used in other recipes by adding them to your extract. If pods were used to flavour a milk or cream in a recipe, just rinse under cold water first. Keep topping up the extract with more vodka as it depletes.

SAVED MY LIFE: REUSING THE SAME VANILLA BEAN

- Real vanilla beans are pricey. So yes, there is an initial start up expense for this recipe, but you can also use recycled vanilla beans (beans used once that have been washed). Real vanilla beans are typically sold in glass vials containing two or three beans, located in the spice aisle or sometimes close to the check out. Try buying them in bulk or ordering online. I have not needed to purchase pure vanilla extract in over 7 years and the quality is undeniable.

EXTRACT TIPS

- I use vodka because of its neutral taste but, by all means, use gin, brandy, rum, bourbon or even just a little splash of one of these mixed in with the vodka. Use any alcohol you like the taste of.
- Some people like to use an overproof (over 50%) alcohol when making extracts; since alcohol is a solvent it will pull out more flavour.

COOL FACT: WHY WE ADD EXTRACTS AT THE END OF RECIPES

When adding extracts to a recipe that involves boiling on a stovetop, always add your extract off the heat at the end of the recipe. The vanilla flavour is held in the alcohol and, when boiled, both the alcohol and the flavour boil off.

(GF, NF, LS)

FRESH HERBY CHEESE BALLS (AKA LABNEH)

Labneh is a popular fresh Middle Eastern cheese made from yogurt. It's simple to make; however, it does require a few days to set. So a wee bit of planning is in order.

Labneh has the most delicate creamy texture, making it the ideal spread for crackers or sandwiches, or as a mid-afternoon snack if you're feeling peckish. It's the star of the show on any cheese board, which is why it's one of my go-tos when entertaining. Anything that impresses my guests but takes me very little effort to make is my kind of entertaining.

MAKES 6 cups (1½ L)
PREP TIME 5 minutes
STAND TIME 3 days
SPECIAL EQUIPMENT NEEDED cheesecloth, fine mesh sieve

1 tsp (5 mL) salt

4 cups (1 L) plain Greek yogurt (2% or more)

1 cup (250 mL) extra virgin olive oil (approx.)

6 black peppercorns

1 clove of garlic, cut into thin slices

4 sprigs fresh herbs, like thyme, tarragon, sage or rosemary

Tart and Smoky Spice Mix (see below; optional)

2 Tbsp (30 mL) chopped fresh herbs (such as chives, tarragon, parsley, dill, cilantro or mint), for garnish

2 Tbsp (30 mL) finely chopped nuts or seeds, for garnish

TART AND SMOKY SPICE MIX

1 Tbsp (15 mL) ground sumac (see Sumac Tip p. 18)

1 Tbsp (15 mL) paprika

1 tsp (5 mL) smoked paprika

1. In a bowl, stir salt into the yogurt.
2. Line a mesh strainer with 2 layers of cheesecloth and set over a bowl. Pour salted yogurt into the cheesecloth and tie up cheesecloth ends. You can leave it like this or you can suspend the bag over the bowl by tying it to something like a pot rack.
3. Leave at room temperature for 3 days. Once the yogurt releases all the excess moisture, it will have the consistency of cream cheese. Remove cheese from the cheesecloth.
4. Fill a jar up with 1 inch (2.5 cm) oil. Add peppercorns, garlic and herbs. Start rolling balls of cheese about the size of walnuts with damp hands. Keep as-is or roll in Tart and Smoky Spice Mix, then gently place in the jar. Top up with more oil as you go. Store in the fridge but let come to room temperature before serving.
5. Serve balls with a little drizzle of herb oil from the jar, or garnish and/or roll in the chopped fresh herbs and nuts suggested.

SAVED MY LIFE: REUSING CHEESECLOTH
Use it, wash it with soap and water, rinse, hang to dry and reuse! Some folks even throw them in the washing machine! You can even boil it for 10 minutes if you have a little germaphobia.

LABNEH TIP

- The leftover infused oil from the labneh can be added to almost everything! Use it in salad dressings, or drizzled over steamed veggies or grilled meats.

(V, GF, NF, LS)

BASIL AND ARUGULA PESTO

Pesto is not just for pasta. Store-bought versions are really quite good but they are never as good as homemade. For scrambled eggs or meat marinades, it's always nice to have a jar of this in my fridge. I love the peppery kick of the arugula and I use walnuts instead of pine nuts because pine nuts are just so darn expensive. For a nut-free version, omit nuts altogether or use seeds like pumpkin or sunflower.

I like to make a big batch of this in the summertime when basil is cheap and abundant. I freeze it in little containers to keep me going through the fall.

For a really great kid-friendly soup try Chicken Soup au Pistou (with Pesto) on page 78.

MAKES 1 cup (250 mL)
COOK TIME 5 minutes
SPECIAL EQUIPMENT NEEDED food processor or mortar and pestle

½ cup (125 mL) nuts or seeds of choice

1 clove garlic, roughly chopped

½ cup (125 mL) freshly grated Parmesan, pecorino Romano cheese or nutritional yeast (see Saved My Life below)

1 cup (250 mL) packed basil

1 cup (250 mL) packed arugula

½ cup (125 mL) parsley

Salt to taste

⅔ cup (160 mL) extra virgin olive oil + extra for container

Pepper to taste

1. Toast walnuts in a dry sauté pan over medium heat, about 3 minutes or until fragrant and slightly browned. Transfer to a bowl to cool slightly.
2. Purée chopped garlic in a food processor or with mortar and pestle. Add toasted nuts and grated cheese (or nutritional yeast) and continue to pulse or grind until you have a coarse paste. Add basil, arugula and parsley, pulsing or grinding with the pestle, scraping down the sides as you go, until herbs break down into a thick green paste. Season with salt. Obviously this takes longer with a mortar and pestle. Pulsing in a food processor takes just a few minutes whereas a mortar and pestle can take up to 10 minutes.
3. With the food processor running, drizzle in olive oil until incorporated, or add olive oil into the mortar. Stir in with the pestle until a paste forms. Taste and adjust seasoning with salt and pepper if necessary.
4. Store in an airtight container with a drizzle of olive oil overtop, or with a layer of plastic wrap touching the surface of the pesto. Both methods help to prevent oxidation, which will discolour the top layer of pesto. Store in the fridge for up to a week or freeze in smaller storage containers for up to 4 months.

SAVED MY LIFE: NUTRITIONAL YEAST

This amazing dairy-free cheese alternative was introduced to me by my vegan friends. They love it because of its high vitamin B content. It looks like larger flaked grated Parmesan and has the slightly salty, nutty and melty quality of Parmesan. My kids love it so I can easily swap it for cheese in certain recipes. It also lasts longer than freshly grated Parmesan and is cheaper. Try it sprinkled on popcorn.

COOL FACT: HOW TO STORE HERBS PROPERLY

While unpacking groceries, wash herbs and shake them dry. Store in a jar with enough water to cover the roots, as you would flowers, then loosely cover in a plastic fruit and vegetable bag. Another method is to wrap the roots in damp paper towels and store in a plastic bag in the fridge. They will last up to 2 weeks like this.

FOUR DIY SPICE MIXES

When you buy spice mixes, sauces and marinades you are buying flavour in convenient packaging. This is not a bad thing. I do it too. I just want to open your mind a little and show you how easy it is to make a fancy spice mix at home. I guarantee it will taste better than anything you buy and they will cost less.

Whole spices stay fresh twice as long as ground ones, and freshly ground spices are intensely better tasting. I dare you to compare the taste of freshly ground cumin to store bought. You probably have all the spices you need in your cupboard to make a great spice rub, you just need to know how to mix them up. Here are my top four.

(V, GF, NF, LS)

HERBES DE PROVENCE

MAKES ½ cup (125 mL)
COOK TIME 5 minutes

2 Tbsp (30 mL) dried thyme

2 Tbsp (30 mL) dried savory

2 Tbsp (30 mL) dried rosemary

1 Tbsp (15 mL) dried oregano or marjoram

1 Tbsp (15 mL) dried lavender

1 tsp (5 mL) anise or fennel seed

1. Mix ingredients and store in a resealable plastic bag or airtight jar for up to 6 months.
2. Use 1–2 Tbsp (15–30 mL) on fish, chicken or meat; sprinkle in stews or bake into bread and buns. Try it with my Easy Herby Cheddar Cheese Biscuits (see p. 145).

(V, GF, NF, LS)

ZA'ATAR

MAKES 6 Tbsp (90 mL)
COOK TIME 5 minutes

2 Tbsp (30 mL) ground sumac

2 Tbsp (30 mL) black and white sesame seeds, any combination

2 Tbsp (30 mL) dried thyme

1. Mix ingredients together in a small bowl and store in a resealable plastic bag or airtight jar for up to 6 months.
2. Sprinkle on anything that needs a savoury, zesty kick, like meat, rice or veggies, or sprinkle in olive oil as a dip for bread. The dark burgundy colour, aroma and tang of sumac will liven up any dish.

SUMAC TIP

Dried sumac berries, sold whole or ground, are typically quite inexpensive, especially if you have a good bulk food or spice store nearby. However, purchasing za'atar in a specialty food store will cost you a pretty penny.

FOUR DIY SPICE MIXES CONTINUED . . .

(V, GF, LS)

DUKKAH

MAKES 2 cups (500 mL)
PREP TIME 5 minutes
COOK TIME 10 minutes
SPECIAL EQUIPMENT NEEDED spice grinder or small food processor or mortar and pestle

- 1½ cups (375 mL) nuts (I like a combination of almonds and pistachios)
- ½ cup (125 mL) black or white sesame seeds, any combination
- 2 Tbsp (30 mL) coriander seeds
- 2 Tbsp (30 mL) cumin seeds
- 1 Tbsp (15 mL) fennel or anise seeds
- 1 tsp (5 mL) turmeric
- 1 tsp (5 mL) chili flakes (optional)
- 1 tsp (5 mL) dried oregano or marjoram
- 1 tsp (5 mL) peppercorns
- 1 tsp (5 mL) salt

1. Toast your nuts by placing them in a dry, medium-sized sauté pan over medium heat. Toss occasionally until fragrant and golden brown, about 3–5 minutes. Once toasted, transfer to a dish to cool, preventing any residual heat from the pan from over-toasting the nuts.
2. Toast seeds in the same pan over medium heat until lightly browned and fragrant, about 2–3 minutes. Transfer to separate small dish.
3. Toast your spices in the same pan over medium heat until fragrant, about 1 minute. Transfer to the dish with the nuts to cool.
4. Once cooled, use a mortar and pestle, grinder or food processor to break up the nuts and spices until you have a coarse mixture.
5. Stir in the salt and sesame seeds and store in an airtight container in the fridge for up to 1 month. For extended storage, freeze.
6. Use as a topping as well as a spice mix, It adds amazing texture when sprinkled on salads and vegetable dishes, it's great on meat and seafood, or try dipping veggies in oil then dunking them in dukkah.

TOASTING NUTS TIPS

- Nuts aren't cheap and burn quickly, so don't get distracted and forget about them. Set a timer if you need to.
- An alternative method for toasting nuts and seeds is to place them on a dry baking sheet in a preheated 350°F (175°C) oven for 8–10 minutes, checking regularly.

(V, GF, NF, LS)

NO SALT-ADDED MEXICAN SPICE MIX

MAKES ½ cup (125 mL)
COOK TIME 5 minutes
SPECIAL EQUIPMENT NEEDED spice grinder or mortar and pestle (if using whole spices)

¼ cup (60 mL) chili powder
1 tsp (5 mL) chili flakes
¼ tsp (1 mL) ground cayenne
2 tsp (10 mL) ground cumin
1 tsp (5 mL) ground coriander
1 tsp (5 mL) garlic powder
1 tsp (5 mL) onion powder
1 tsp (5 mL) paprika
2 tsp (10 mL) smoked paprika
1 tsp (5 mL) dried oregano

1. Mix all ingredients together and store in a resealable plastic bag or airtight jar for up to 6 months.
2. I use about 4 tsp (20 mL) spice mix per 1 lb (450 g) meat, poultry or other vegetarian substitution.

SPICE TIP

- Toasting spices before grinding them gives them a big flavour boost.

(V, GF, NF, LS)

AA BUTTER

I remember the days when my kids were babies and I used to make them homemade applesauce. Looking back, I wish I had known about this recipe. Having a few jars of this silky sweet, no sugar-added sauce packed away would have been a lifesaver. No butter, apple peeling or effort associated with this recipe. The slow cooker does all the work.

Eat it with a spoon, spread it on toast or pair it with something savoury like a pork or turkey dish.

MAKES five to six 1-cup (250 mL) jars
PREP TIME 10 minutes
COOK TIME 5–6 hours
SPECIAL EQUIPMENT NEEDED slow cooker, food processor or blender

- 2 lb (900 g) apples, quartered (I like to use a combination of sweet and tart, like honeycrisp and Granny Smith)
- 2 lb (900 g) apricots, halved
- ¼ cup (60 mL) water
- ½ cinnamon stick
- ½ vanilla bean, cut in half and sliced lengthwise
- Pinch of salt
- Fresh lemon juice to taste (optional)

1. Place apples, apricots, water, cinnamon, vanilla bean and salt in your slow cooker. This should fill a standard-sized slow cooker. Set slow cooker to high for 5 hours. Mash fruit halfway through cooking time.
2. After 5 hours of slow cooking, open lid and cook an additional 45–60 minutes, until colour darkens and most of the liquid evaporates. Check and stir occasionally, consistency should be thick and saucy.
3. Let cool slightly, remove vanilla bean (save, wash and reuse—see Saved My Life on p. 14) and cinnamon stick and transfer to a food processor or blender. Process until you have a buttery, silky-smooth purée, emulsifying all the skins. Taste and adjust seasoning with lemon juice, if you like.
4. Transfer to clean jars, seal, label, date and refrigerate. This will keep for several weeks in the fridge. For canning (see instructions p. 12–13), process for 10 minutes in a boiling-water canner.

AA BUTTER TIPS

- No peeking! We all want to see what's going on in there, but as soon as you open the lid steam escapes, the temperature drops and you can add an extra 20 minutes to your cooking time.
- If you feel as though your butter is still too watery after puréeing, put it back in the slow cooker (or even a saucepot over medium-low heat) with the lid open for an extra 15–20 minutes, stirring occasionally until thickened.

COOL FACT: NOT ALL APPLES COOK THE SAME

Apples have two main distinguishing features when used in cooking: soft, which are the ones that turn mushy when cooked and are best used for things like applesauce (ex. McIntosh), or hard, which are the ones that hold their shape when cooked, like Golden Delicious. The latter are best used in pies and tarts.

(V, GF, NF, LS)

GLUTEN-FREE ALL-PURPOSE FLOUR

When it comes to gluten-free baking, I like to make my own flour blend. This way I know exactly how it works, giving me consistency in all of my baking and bread recipes.

The sorghum flour adds stability and "muscle," the potato starch keeps everything light and fluffy without drying it out and the tapioca flour adds the perfect chewy texture.

I replace this flour cup for cup, but since the required amount of xanthan gum changes depending on what you're making, I add it separately (see amounts below the ingredients in this recipe).

When purchasing gluten-free all-purpose flours double check to see if xanthan gum is already mixed in or you have to do it yourself. I've had many friends wonder why their gluten-free baking is not working until they realized they needed to add xanthan gum.

MAKES 4 cups (1 L)
COOK TIME 5 minutes
SPECIAL EQUIPMENT NEEDED sifter or fine mesh sieve

1½ cups (375 mL) sorghum flour

1½ cups (375 mL) potato starch (not potato flour)

1 cup (250 mL) tapioca flour or starch

Xanthan gum (see Cool Fact below)

XANTHAN GUM MEASUREMENTS

¾ tsp (4 mL) per 1 cup (250 mL) flour for bread and dough recipes

½ tsp (2 mL) per 1 cup (250 mL) flour for other baking recipes

1. Mix all ingredients except xanthan gum together in a large bowl. Use a whisk at first, then sift the flour mix into another bowl to ensure everything is evenly incorporated.
2. Store in a resealable plastic bag or airtight container. I do suggest labelling it, especially if your pantry looks anything like mine. Lasts up to 3 months, or place in freezer for extended use.
3. Whisk xanthan gum into your flour before incorporating into a recipe.

SAVED MY LIFE: SORGHUM

I love sorghum. Not only milled as flour, but as my go-to gluten-free super grain, like in my Sweet and Spicy Spaghetti Squash with Sorghum recipe (see p. 110). It is naturally high in iron, fibre, protein, magnesium, potassium—the list goes on and on. It is also inexpensive to buy. For a cool treat, pop the grains the same as you would popcorn. You'll get mini popcorn with a nutty flavour twist.

GLUTEN-FREE FLOUR TIPS

- If you can't find these ingredients in your local grocery store I recommend the nearest natural food or bulk food store.
- Be careful not to confuse potato starch and potato flour. Potato flour will taste like potatoes while the starch is neutral. You want the starch.
- Tapioca flour is cheap and easily found in the Asian section of your grocery store or any Asian market.
- Forgetful like me? Write the xanthan gum measurements needed on the container your flour is stored in, as a reminder.

COOL FACT: WHY IS XANTHAN GUM ADDED?

This fine white powder is used as a thickener or to create elasticity and firmness in baked goods. It is powerful in small quantities, which is why you need only a tiny bit. When buying gluten-free flour mixes make sure to check and see if the xanthan gum is added in already or not. You don't want to double it up, but you also don't want to leave it out.

(V, GF, NF, LS)

HOMEMADE HOT SAUCE

In our house, hot sauce is as common as salt and pepper. It is, in a way, addictive. You develop a taste and tolerance for the heat and flavour profiles of different chili peppers. This is a very good thing. Not only can hot sauces boast almost unbelievable health benefits such as curing depression and lowering blood pressure, they are also my number one way to boost flavour in bland foods without adding fat and calories.

MAKES enough for 4 small mason jars
PREP TIME 15 minutes
COOK TIME 20 minutes
SPECIAL EQUIPMENT NEEDED food processor or blender, 4 small mason jars with lids, latex or rubber kitchen gloves

24 hot peppers of choice (I like a mix of jalapenos and long red chilies)

1 Tbsp (15 mL) neutral tasting oil

½ red onion chopped

2 cloves garlic, chopped

2 Tbsp (30 mL) maple syrup or honey (more if desired)

1 cup (250 mL) water

Salt to taste

¾ cup (185 mL) white vinegar (more if desired)

1. Cut hot peppers in half lengthwise, discarding stems, seeds and inner ribs (which hold the most heat), then roughly chop. I highly recommended wearing gloves. The peppers' intense heat will permeate into your skin and transfer onto anything you touch. You won't notice this until it's too late, like when you rub your eyes or go the bathroom. Also make sure to wash your knife, all utensils and the cutting board after processing the peppers.

2. Place a medium-sized saucepot over medium heat. Add the oil and sauté the onion until translucent, about 3 minutes. Add garlic and continue to cook over medium for another 2–3 minutes, being careful not to burn the garlic.

3. Add hot peppers, 2 Tbsp (30 mL) maple syrup, water and a pinch of salt to saucepot. Bring to a boil, lower heat and let simmer for 20 minutes, stirring occasionally. Also, it's not the best idea to breathe in the aroma of simmering hot sauce. Set aside to cool.

4. Transfer mixture into a food processor or blender and purée. While puréeing, slowly drizzle in ¾ cup (185 mL) vinegar, tasting along the way. Adjust seasonings to your liking by adding more vinegar, salt or maple syrup.

5. Transfer to clean mason jars, label and date. Store in the refrigerator for up to 6 months. Wash food processor immediately!

SAVED MY LIFE: AN AVOCADO, HOT SAUCE AND A SPOON

One of my favourite healthy on-the-go snacks is half an avocado, sprinkled with a pinch of salt then drizzled with homemade hot sauce.

HOT SAUCE TIP

- Keep it simple if you like it hot. The more you add to a hot sauce, like different seasonings or flavours, the more heat you take away. Remember, the most famous hot sauces use only hot peppers, salt and vinegar.

COOL FACT: HOW IS HEAT MEASURED?

The spicy heat or "capsaicin" from chilies is measured in Scoville scale units. Jalapenos sit low on the scale at 10,000 units, whereas habaneros and bird's eye chilies are much higher on this scale, between 100,000 and 350,000 units. Choose your hot peppers wisely.

(V, GF, LS)

VANILLA ALMOND MILK

I love making my own nut and seed milks for a variety of reasons: the organic versions at the grocery store are expensive, and the commercial brands can be loaded with sugar and additives. Making my own is easy, affordable and, when it comes to flavour, the possibilities are endless.

I love to substitute nut and seed milks in my baking recipes, smoothies and coffee, and they are a great flavour booster in my morning porridge.

The bonus of this recipe is the leftover pulp, which can easily be turned into flour, either in the oven or in a dehydrator (see Almond Milk Tips below). It is also easy to sneak in ½ cup (125 mL) of damp leftover pulp into a pancake or waffle recipe.

MAKES 4 cups (1 L)
PREP TIME 2 minutes
STAND TIME 8–12 hours
SPECIAL EQUIPMENT NEEDED really good blender, nut milk bag or cheesecloth, one 4-cup (1 L) glass jar with lid (like a glass milk jug)

- 1 cup (250 mL) almonds
- 4 cups (1 L) cold water
- 2 tsp (10 mL) Pure Vanilla Extract (see p. 14)
- Pinch of salt (optional)

1. Cover almonds with water in a covered container for 8–12 hours, or overnight.
2. Drain and rinse well in a colander. Place almonds in a blender with 4 cups (1 L) cold water, vanilla and salt, if using. Using the high setting, blend until as smooth as possible, 1–3 minutes. Strain milk through a strainer lined with a double layer of cheesecloth, or through a nut milk bag draped over a bowl. Twisting fabric from the top down, strain out as much liquid as possible.
3. Pour into a clean glass container, and keep refrigerated for up to 1 week.
4. Store-bought milks have emulsifiers and stabilizers that prevent the milk from separating. It is totally normal for homemade nut and seed milks to separate. Just give it a good shake before using.

SAVED MY LIFE: BUYING IN BULK AND STORING NUTS IN MY FREEZER (FOR LONGER SHELF LIFE)

I don't know how many times I have gotten home late from work only to find an empty carton of milk on the counter. The last thing I want to do is leave the house and go to the store. Since I buy most things in bulk, there is likely a cup of nuts in my freezer at any given time. I can soak them overnight and make fresh nut milk in the morning.

ALMOND MILK TIPS

- Try adding in 2 tsp (10 mL) honey or 4 drops stevia extract to sweeten the milk, and a dash of cinnamon and/or nutmeg to enhance flavours while blending.
- Use this milk as a replacement for dairy in most recipes.
- Nut milk bags are cheap and easily found online or in any health food shop.
- Leftover pulp can be reused! For the super frugal and adventurous, dehydrate pulp and make it into flour; 4 hours at 115°F (45°C) in a dehydrator or 2 hours at 200°F (95°C) in a conventional oven. Cool and then blend in a food processor to make flour.

COOL FACT: HOW TO MAKE OTHER NUT MILKS

Use the same proportions and method for cashews, macadamia nuts, Brazil nuts or hazelnuts.

(GF, NF, LS)

ORANGE SUMAC YOGURT DIP

It's nice to have one cool yogurt dip in your repertoire when you are looking for that little zing to top almost anything. You probably have an orange and some yogurt kicking around your fridge. Sumac, ok, maybe not, but if and when you get your hands on this zesty spice, you will see how it breathes life into any dish. You can buy it whole or ground in any bulk food or spice store. It is relatively inexpensive and you will use it over and over again.

I make this recipe with homemade yogurt but if you want something denser, try Greek-style yogurt.

Try this dip with my Super Juicy Turkey Sliders (see p. 109) or my Roast Sweet Potato Coins with Thyme (see p. 93). It's also a welcome companion to any Mediterranean or curry dinner.

MAKES ½ cup (125 mL)
COOK TIME 5 minutes

- ½ cup (125 mL) plain yogurt
- 1 tsp (5 mL) orange zest
- 1 Tbsp (15 mL) freshly squeezed orange juice
- 1 Tbsp (15 mL) extra virgin olive oil
- ½ clove garlic, puréed
- 2 tsp (10 mL) ground sumac (see Sumac Tip p. 18)
- Salt to taste
- Pepper to taste

1. Stir all ingredients together in a bowl and store in an airtight container in the fridge.

SAVED MY LIFE: A MICROPLANE

This was one of the required utensils for culinary school. I never had one before school and now I have three. It makes puréeing garlic, zesting citrus and grating that cumbersome ginger a snap. No pun intended. I use mine every day.

CITRUS ZESTING TIPS

- Maybe obvious, but zest the citrus first, then juice the fruit.
- If using citrus zest, buy organic if you can. If not, wash very well. The thick skins will have traces of pesticides and are sometimes treated with chemicals to maintain freshness.
- You get more juice from room-temperature citrus. Also, roll citrus fruit between your hand and the cutting board to help release juices.

(V, GF, NF, LS)

CHEAP AND SIMPLE SAUERKRAUT

Sauerkraut and other raw fermentations have become very trendy food items, but buying a bottle of sauerkraut these days can put a dent in your wallet. There are certain things I cannot justify spending money on and sauerkraut is one of them. It couldn't be easier to make: cabbage is super cheap all year round and one whole head can keep you well-krauted for a few months. The only thing sauerkraut requires is a little patience.

Besides eating it straight from the jar, I love sprinkling it on salads, tacos, mixed in with rice or on my recipe for Heirloom Carrot and Spicy Sauerkraut Quinoa Salad (see p. 72).

MAKES enough for one 4-cup (1 L) mason jar
PREP TIME 15 minutes
FERMENTATION TIME 3–13 days
SPECIAL EQUIPMENT NEEDED 4-cup (1 L) mason jar (preferably with a wide-mouth), cheesecloth

- 1 head green cabbage (about 2 lb/900 g)
- ¼ cup (60 mL) whey (optional; if not using add an extra 1 Tbsp/15 mL salt)
- 1 Tbsp (15 mL) salt
- ½ tsp (2 mL) dill seeds
- ½ tsp (2 mL) fennel seeds
- 1 Tbsp (15 mL) dried marjoram or oregano
- ½–1 tsp (2–5 mL) dried chili flakes (optional)

1. Remove outer leaves of the cabbage, quarter, remove core and thinly slice. Place cabbage in large bowl and sprinkle over all remaining ingredients. Set aside 1 outer leaf to place on top of the kraut when fermenting.
2. Squeeze and massage cabbage with clean hands (or pound with a meat hammer) until cabbage looks wet and wilted, about 7–10 minutes. It should have a similar appearance to coleslaw.
3. Spoon cabbage and any remaining juices into a clean 4-cup (1 L) mason jar, pressing down with the end of a wooden spoon as you go. Once juices cover the top of the cabbage, place the reserved cabbage leaf overtop, leaving at least a 1-inch (2.5 cm) space between the top of the cabbage and the top of the jar to prevent bubbles and liquid created during fermentation from overflowing.
4. Cover with lid, place jar in a bowl (to catch any liquid that may overflow) and leave at room temperature in a cool dark place.
5. After 24 hours, check sauerkraut. Unscrew lid to release any pressure and push cabbage down further with clean hands, making sure it is completely covered with liquid. Let ferment another 2 days.
6. Unscrew jar and watch the bubbles percolate. Fermentation! Sauerkraut can be eaten right away. I prefer it less salty, so I like to leave it for an additional 7–10 days. You should start to notice the cabbage change from mild green to translucent.
7. Transfer to the refrigerator. Sauerkraut gets yummier with time.

SAUERKRAUT TIPS

- Get a little more creative on your next batch: replace a portion of the cabbage with grated carrots, sliced onion or fennel.
- Sometimes the cabbage on top of the jar browns from contact with the air. This is completely normal. Just skim off and throw away. Push cabbage further down until covered with liquid again. You can also top up the jar with a little more water if necessary.

COOL FACT: WHY THE WHEY?

Whey is added to create lacto-fermentation. It helps preserve food and contains beneficial lactobacilli, which is good stuff for your gut.

To make whey, place plain yogurt in a strainer lined with 2 layers of cheesecloth fit over a bowl. Collect ¼ cup (60 mL) of the whey and reserve thickened yogurt for another use. You can also fold the edges of the cheesecloth overtop and place in the fridge overnight to create a Greek-style yogurt. No whey? Just add an additional 1 Tbsp (15 mL) of salt.

(V, GF, NF)

VANILLA, PLUM AND RHUBARB JAM

There needed to be one jam recipe in this book, for the sake of tradition only. I make jam every year, the same as my mother did, the same as her mother did (I think). The nostalgia alone of opening up a jar in the dead of winter to smell and taste the flavours of rhubarb plucked from my backyard is reason enough to make at least one batch of homemade jam.

It is up to you whether or not you want to actually seal the jars in a boiling-water canner, or just make a batch to give to friends or eat right away. I have provided methods for both.

MAKES enough for five to six 1-cup (250 mL) jam jars
PREP TIME 5 minutes
COOK TIME 10 minutes
SPECIAL EQUIPMENT NEEDED boiling-water canner (optional), boiling-water canning kit (optional), jam jars, ring bands (which can be reused), new lids (can't be reused), digital thermometer or 3 spoons (see Jam Tips below)

- 1 vanilla bean, split lengthwise
- 2½ cups (625 mL) rhubarb stalks, chopped into 1-inch (2.5 cm) chunks
- 2½ cups (625 mL) yellow plums, washed, pits removed and cubed
- 2 cups (500 mL) sugar (or to taste)
- Juice of 1 lemon
- Pinch of salt

1. If canning, prepare boiling-water canner by filling it with water and bringing to a boil. Sterilize jars in boiling water for 10 minutes or run jars through a hot cycle in your dishwasher. Heat new lids in a small pot of hot water, do not boil. Set aside jar bands. Jars and lids should be kept warm until ready to use.
2. Scrape seeds from inside the vanilla bean. Toss pod, seeds and all other remaining ingredients into a large thick-bottomed saucepot. Bring to simmer over medium heat, stirring occasionally, until thickened and fruit is cooked to jellying stage at 220°F (103°C), about 20 minutes. (Don't have digital thermometer? See Jam Tips below.)
3. Ladle into sterilized jars leaving a ¼-inch (6 mm) space between the lid and contents of the jar. Clean rim with a damp paper towel and, if not processing, seal and store in the fridge for up to 3 weeks. If processing, process for 10 minutes following the instructions on page 12-13.

SAVED MY LIFE: BUYING A DIGITAL SCALE

Having a digital scale meant I no longer had to search to convert ingredients from volume to mass. I could look at any recipe no matter how it was written and know that I could quickly weigh ingredients out correctly. The added bonus was that I could weigh everything in one bowl or pot just by zeroing out the previous measurements. Less dishes to clean makes me very happy.

When looking to buy a digital scale, look for one that easily switches between metric and imperial measurements, that you can clean easily and that turns off automatically.

JAM TIPS

- Did you know that slightly unripe fruit mixed in with ripe fruit make the best jam? Unripe fruit contains more pectin and will make for a better consistency in the end.
- No digital thermometer? Take a few spoons and place them in the freezer. Test jam after it has simmered for 15 minutes by taking one frozen spoon, drizzling some jam onto it, waiting a few seconds for it to cool, then sliding a finger through the jam. If you see a clean line through the jam, without it filling in, then you're done. If not, boil for another few minutes and try again with another spoon.

(GF, NF, LS)

ONE-MINUTE MAYO

I have no problem eating raw eggs, but when I do (or if I am serving raw eggs to my kids) I use the freshest eggs possible. Unless you are lucky enough to have a chicken coop in your backyard, buy pasteurized eggs.

If making homemade mayo tastes so much better (it does!), and only takes a minute, then the only reason you are buying it from a store is because of its shelf life. We don't go through a lot of mayonnaise in our house so I never really buy it, but I use this recipe for special occasions, like a family barbecue or dinner party.

MAKES a little over 1 cup (250 mL)
COOK TIME 1 minute
SPECIAL EQUIPMENT NEEDED food processor or blender

1 egg, preferably pasteurized

2 tsp (10 mL) white wine vinegar or fresh lemon juice

1 tsp (5 mL) Dijon mustard

½ tsp (2 mL) salt

Pepper to taste

1 cup (250 mL) neutral-flavoured oil

OPTIONAL ADDITIVES

1 canned chipotle in adobo, finely chopped

1–2 tsp (5–10 mL) chili powder

A few dashes of your favourite hot sauce

1–2 tsp (5–10 mL) prepared horseradish

1 Tbsp (15 mL) finely chopped herbs, such as tarragon, chives, cilantro or basil

1 clove puréed garlic and 1 Tbsp (15 mL) lemon zest

1. Place egg, vinegar (or lemon juice), mustard, salt, pepper and any additional ingredients you choose into a food processor or blender.
2. Pulse, then add oil in a slow steady stream; count to 30 seconds, or until oil is completely emulsified and you have a thick creamy mayo.
3. Taste and adjust seasoning if necessary. Store in an airtight container or glass jar with a lid for 7 days, if it doesn't get used up before then. You will find yourself dipping everything into that mayo.

COOL FACT: YOU CAN SUSPEND OIL IN WATER

Water and oil do not mix; however, you can suspend oil in water (such as with mayonnaise or creams) and water in oil (like in vinaigrettes) through emulsification. This is why we must beat, shake or slowly whisk oil to create tiny beads of oil suspended in water, like in this mayonnaise recipe.

(V, GF, NF, LS)

MY CLASSIC FRENCH VINAIGRETTE

I grew up on iceberg lettuce salads drizzled with vegetable oil, white vinegar, salt and pepper. This bare-boned salad was much loved and I can remember eating full heads of iceberg lettuce swimming in this homely dressing. So it makes sense to me that all a salad needs is a great, simple dressing. I want to taste my salad, not have it swimming in some sugary concoction.

There is also nothing worse than too much raw garlic in a salad dressing, so trust me on the half clove of puréed garlic. If it is a big clove, just purée one quarter of it. Your guests will thank you for it.

MAKES ½ cup (125 mL) or enough for 1 large salad
COOK TIME 5 minutes

½ clove garlic, puréed

1 Tbsp (15 mL) Dijon mustard

1 Tbsp (15 mL) white wine or apple cider vinegar

Pinch of salt

⅓ cup (80 mL) neutral-flavoured or extra virgin olive oil (approx; see Cool Fact)

Pepper to taste

1 tsp (5 mL) honey, maple syrup or your favourite jam (optional)

1. In a small bowl, combine garlic, mustard, vinegar and salt with a small whisk or fork.
2. Slowly drizzle in the oil, while whisking, until you have a thick creamy vinaigrette. Taste and season with more salt or pepper.

SAVED MY LIFE: HOW I FINALLY GOT MY KIDS TO EAT SALADS

This is an honest cookbook, so here it is. When the kids were toddlers I went and bought a whole bunch of different store-bought dressings. When I made a salad or put out raw vegetables before dinner I would let them experiment. I let them choose. After a while they gravitated towards the classics, mostly simple vinaigrettes. Over time, it dwindled down to one favourite, which was actually labelled "French Vinaigrette." Now they make this homemade vinaigrette themselves whenever we make a salad. Sometime things just take time.

VINAIGRETTE TIPS

- Salad dressing will have a hard time sticking to wet lettuce. The dryer the greens, the better. This is where a salad spinner comes in handy.
- Always dress your salad just before serving so the leaves stay crisp.
- A vinaigrette may separate if made in advance. If it does, give it a good shake in a mason jar or whisk until emulsified.

COOL FACT: DIFFERENT OILS CREATE DIFFERENT FLAVOURS

Since this is my all-time favourite salad dressing, the only thing I fiddle with is the oil. It is amazing how 1 Tbsp (15 mL) of pumpkin seed, walnut or sesame oil can add variety to the vinaigrette's flavour. Nut and seed oils (sometimes called "finishing" oils) are typically strong in flavour, so don't replace all the oil in your salad dressing with them. Start by adding 1 Tbsp (15 mL) nut/seed oil along with a neutral tasting oil (for a total of ⅓ cup/80 mL). I have a few of these fancier finishing oils in my fridge (delicate oils stay fresher longer in the fridge), mostly to flavour my vinaigrettes.

FOUR SIMPLE STOCKS

The best thing about making any stock is that the process is very forgiving. You can follow the measurements exactly or do what I do and just eyeball it.

The term broth and stock are used interchangeably. There is a difference between the two (broths are made from bones and meat, whereas stocks are made from only bones), but in my world and throughout this cookbook they are one in the same. I use the word "stock" to describe both.

When making a stock, I think in ratios instead of actual amounts. Everyone has a different size of stockpot so I just fill a pot with bones, add cold water to cover the bones by 2 inches (5 cm) and start simmering. Then I add my mirepoix (a fancy word for an aromatic vegetable mixture that includes 2 parts onion, 1 part carrot and 1 part celery) and other veggies and/or flavourings as I go. Fresh herbs I typically add during the last 45 minutes of simmering.

The general rule of thumb for making vegetable stock is to have equal parts onion, carrot and celery. You want to avoid too much of one vegetable and keep bitter greens to a minimum (kale, collard, mustard greens and radishes) so as not to overpower the stock. Beets and purple cabbage will turn everything dark reddish/purple, which is sometimes cool.

(GF, NF, LS)

WHITE STOCK

MAKES 16 cups (4 L)
PREP TIME 5 minutes
COOK TIME 4–8 hours (stovetop) or 24 hours (crockpot)
SPECIAL EQUIPMENT NEEDED crockpot (optional)

6 lb (2.7 kg) bones (chicken, veal, beef or game bird; see note p. 35), washed and uncooked

16 cups (4 L) cold water

17 oz (500 g) raw mirepoix, large dice

Additional vegetables (shallots, leeks, garlic, fennel, celeriac, parsnip, mushrooms, etc) to taste

2–3 bay leaves

Small bunch parsley stems

5 springs thyme

½ Tbsp (7 mL) peppercorns

⅓ cup (80 mL) apple cider vinegar or ½ cup (125 mL) white wine

Seasonings (oregano, ginger, lovage, lemongrass, tarragon, rosemary; use sparingly!) to taste

1. Fill a stockpot with bones, add cold water to cover the bones by 2 inches (5 cm) and bring to a simmer. Skim at this point if needed.
2. Add mirepoix, other veggies and/or seasonings and vinegar or wine. Continue to simmer.
3. If using beef or veal bones, cook for 6–8 hours on the stovetop, or 24 hours in a crockpot. For chicken bones, cook for 4 hours on the stovetop or 24 hours in a crockpot. Skim along the way.
4. Strain. portion and store in the fridge or freezer.

(GF, NF, LS)

BROWN STOCK

MAKES 16 cups (4 L)
PREP TIME 20 minutes for roasting bones
COOK TIME 4–8 hours (stovetop) or 24 hours (crockpot)
SPECIAL EQUIPMENT NEEDED crockpot (optional)

6 lb (2.7 kg) bones (roasted chicken, veal, beef or game bones; see note p. 35)

16 cups (4 L) cold water

17 oz (500 g) mirepoix, large dice, preferably roasted

Additional vegetables (celeriac, mushrooms, garlic, shallots, leeks, parsnips, tomatoes) to taste or 6 oz (175 g) tomato paste

Small bunch parsley stems

2–3 bay leaves

5 sprigs fresh thyme

½ Tbsp (7 mL) peppercorns

Additional seasonings (1 whole clove, rosemary, oregano; use sparingly) to taste

⅓ cup (80 mL) apple cider vinegar or ½ cup (125 mL) red wine

1. Fill a stockpot with roasted bones, add cold water to cover the bones by 2 inches (5 cm) and bring to a simmer. Skim at this point if needed.
2. Add browned mirepoix, other veggies and/or seasonings, vinegar or wine. Continue to simmer.
3. Simmer 6–8 hours on the stovetop, or 24 hours in a crockpot. For only chicken bones, cook for 4 hours on the stovetop or 24 hours in a crockpot. Skim along the way.
4. Strain, portion and store in the fridge or freezer.

(GF, NF, LS)

FISH STOCK

MAKES 16 cups (4 L)
PREP TIME 5 minutes
COOK TIME 45 minutes

9 oz (270 g) chopped mirepoix

2 oz (60 g) mushrooms (or trimmings)

Additional vegetables (leeks, shallots, fennel, garlic) to taste

1 Tbsp (15 mL) butter or olive oil

6 lb (2.7 kg) lean fish bones (see note p. 35)

½–1 cup (125–250 mL) white wine

16 cups (4 L) cold water

2–3 bay leaves

½ Tbsp (7 mL) peppercorns

Additional Seasonings (thyme, tarragon, lemongrass, ginger) to taste

1. In a large stockpot, sauté the mirepoix and vegetables in oil or butter until softened. Add in bones and cover over low heat until bones are opaque.
2. Deglaze with white wine, add in water and remaining ingredients. Bring to boil, skim and lower to simmer for 30–45 minutes.
3. Strain, portion and store in the fridge or freezer.

(GF, NF, LS)

VEGETABLE STOCK

MAKES 16 cups (4 L)
PREP TIME 5 minutes
COOK TIME 45 minutes

26 oz (750 g) equal parts chopped onions, carrots and celery

Additional vegetables (tomatoes, leeks, parsnip, garlic, mushrooms, fennel, celeriac, shallots, parsnips) to taste

1–2 Tbsp (15–30 mL) olive oil

2–3 bay leaves

½ Tbsp (7 mL) peppercorns

Small bunch of parsley stems

5 sprigs thyme

Additional seasonings (oregano, lovage, garlic, ginger) to taste

16 cups (4 L) cold water

1. In a stockpot, sauté vegetables in oil over medium-high heat until softened. Add all other ingredients, cover with cold water and let simmer for 45 minutes.
2. Strain, portion and store in the fridge or freezer.

BEST BONES TO USE

BEEF/VEAL/GAME Knuckles, shank, marrow, neck bones. Bones with a high percent of cartilage, connective tissue and collagen are the best. This converts to gelatin when cooking, which is what adds richness and body to a stock.

CHICKEN Necks, backs, breastbones and wings. Basically the whole chicken carcass can be used.

FISH Bones from lean fish such as sole, halibut or cod. Bones from fatty fish such as salmon or tuna will produce a stock that tastes like the fish that the bones were taken from. Lean fish provide a more general-purpose stock.

GOLDEN RULES OF MAKING A STOCK

- Always use cold water.
- Simmer, never boil.
- Skim the stock.
- Never add salt.

SAVED MY LIFE: FINDING EASY WAYS TO USE UP EVERYTHING

Make Stone Soup! If you don't already know the tale, Stone Soup is the story of how a fantastic meal can be made from nothing but a fire, pot, water and a stone—or rather, by gathering up a little bit of everything. It is always better than stock you buy at the grocery store, and because you're making it out of scraps you would throw away anyway, it's free! Free stock! I find it hard to throw food away, and this is the absolute best way to use up scraps. Onion skins and ends, carrot peels, celery stumps, wilted herbs, ginger knobs, un-waxed turnip ends, leeks, garlic, lemongrass, fennel scraps and mushroom stems are all really great Stone Soup ingredients. Place a large resealable bag in your freezer and start filling it up over time with your scraps. I guarantee that every time you take out your bag of frozen vegetable scraps to make a stock you will give yourself a pat on the back.

THE MORNING RUSH (AKA BREAKFAST)

I have a hard enough time getting myself up in the mornings, let alone getting the rest of the family out of the house in one piece. Mornings are, by far, the hardest part of my day, and breakfast, being the most important meal of the day, is therefore the most challenging. As much as I would like to paint the perfect family picture of everything being hunky-dory, there is not a week that goes by where someone does not leave the house in a huff. Here is a chapter I hope will make your mornings a little more manageable (as they do mine).

(V, GF, NF, LS)

TREMENDOUS BREAKFAST PORRIDGE

Morning is the busiest time of day in my house, but that doesn't mean breakfast has to take a back seat. Hot or cold, this porridge is ideal because you can make a big batch on the weekend and ensure that it's ready to go any day of the week.

This recipe is nothing like the boring old oatmeal I ate as a kid. Made with quinoa, buckwheat and amaranth, this protein-packed breakfast will help kick-start your day and keep your brain working at maximum capacity—at least until lunchtime.

No sugar is added to this recipe, since I find a handful of dried fruit adds just enough sweetness. Feel free to mix in a drizzle of maple syrup or honey.

MAKES 4 servings
PREP TIME 3 minutes
COOK TIME 13 minutes

- ½ cup (125 mL) quinoa
- ½ cup (125 mL) large flaked rolled oats
- ½ cup (125 mL) raw buckwheat groats
- ½ cup (125 mL) amaranth
- 2 cups (500 mL) water or milk
- 1 tsp (5 mL) ground cinnamon or ½ cinnamon stick
- ½ tsp (2 mL) ground ginger
- ¼ tsp (1 mL) freshly grated nutmeg
- 1 star anise
- Pinch of salt
- Handful of dried cranberries, cherries, blueberries, chopped figs, dates or apricots (optional)

1. Measure all ingredients into a medium-sized saucepot. Place over medium heat and bring to a boil, reduce to simmer, cover and let cook for 13 minutes. Remove from heat and let stand 5 minutes.
2. Serve as is or make porridge parfaits by layering the porridge, yogurt and fresh fruit in mason jars. Assemble the night before for a grab-and-go breakfast.

SAVED MY LIFE: THANK GOODNESS MY KIDS LIKE QUINOA

There is a reason why whole cookbooks have been written about this super seed, and the demand for it over the years has increased its price. It is a gluten-free complete protein, takes 13 minutes to make and can be eaten morning, noon and night. My kids like it simple, just like their rice, with some butter, salt and pepper.

PORRIDGE TIP

- If you love pumpkin pie like I do, try this variation. Replace 1 cup (250 mL) of the cooking liquid with puréed pumpkin or sweet potato purée and add an additional ½ cup (125 mL) water or milk. Naturally sweet and fibre-rich, it is the perfect addition to your morning routine.

COOL FACTS: GLUTEN-FREE GRAINS ARE EASY TO USE

Gluten-free grains like buckwheat groats and amaranth (which are actually seeds) can easily be substituted for other grains. Groats are very mild in taste and are considered a complete protein. Amaranth looks like teeny little seeds and is also highly nutritious. Both can be eaten raw and cook easily.

(V, GF, NF)

NUTTY SEEDY GRANOLA

Granola is a cereal that really knows how to multitask.

I like to eat mine with homemade nut milk (see p. 26) for breakfast, but there are a million other ways you'll want to try it: sprinkle it over yogurt and fruit in the morning, eat it as a snack after the gym, pack it for hungry kids in the car or just sprinkle it over ice cream for dessert. Basically any time of day is granola time.

What makes this the best homemade granola? I have scaled back on the oats and loaded it with more nuts and seeds. Plus you are going to love the flavour combination of raw honey, maple syrup and orange oil.

MAKES 8 cups (2 L)
PREP TIME 15 minutes
COOK TIME 1 hour
SPECIAL EQUIPMENT NEEDED very large bowl

½ cup (125 mL) honey

¼ cup (60 mL) maple syrup

¼ cup (60 mL) water

2 Tbsp (30 mL) coconut oil

1 Tbsp (15 mL) Pure Vanilla Extract (see p. 14)

1 Tbsp (15 mL) orange oil

1 tsp (5 mL) salt

4 cups (1 L) large flake oats

1 cup (250 mL) raw almonds, roughly chopped

1 cup (250 mL) raw pecans, roughly chopped

1 cup (250 mL) raw pumpkin seeds

¼ cup (60 mL) raw sesame seeds

¼ cup (60 mL) raw sunflowers seeds

¼ cup (60 mL) flax seeds

¼ cup (60 mL) chia seeds

½ cup (125 mL) unsweetened large flake coconut

1. Preheat oven to 275°F (140°C) and line a large baking sheet.
2. In a small saucepot over medium heat, stir together the honey, maple syrup, water and coconut oil until free flowing and the coconut oil is completely melted.
3. Remove saucepot from heat and stir in the vanilla extract, orange oil and salt. Set aside.
4. In a very large bowl, toss together the oats, nuts, seeds and coconut. Pour syrup overtop and stir to coat all dry ingredients. Get your hands in there and taste it.
5. Transfer to a lined baking sheet and flatten to create an even layer about ½ inch (1 cm) thick.
6. Bake for 1 hour. Let granola cool completely and break apart into chunks. Store in airtight containers.

SAVED MY LIFE: SILICON BAKING MAT

Non-stick silicon mats come in a range of sizes and can be used over and over again. Using a silicon mat means you don't have to grease a baking sheet or use parchment paper. They aren't cheap but last forever (up to 3,000 uses), clean and store easily and they're dishwasher safe. I deem them a very good investment and one of the best gift-giving ideas for anyone who loves to bake. Commonly called Silpats, an actual French brand, they (and many other knock offs) are easily found in any kitchenware supply store.

GRANOLA TIPS

- Love dried fruit in your granola? Always add dried fruit after you bake the granola. Dried fruit and hot ovens do not mix well. Those lovely bits of chewy sweetness will dry up into little charred clumps if left in the oven for an hour. Toss in 1 cup (250 mL) dried cherries, chopped mango, pineapple or blueberries once the granola has cooled.
- Over the years I have learned that if I mix mini chocolate chips into anything, kids will eat it. A chocolate and dried fruit granola mix is perfect for long road trips, hikes or any time that you need a good snack on hand that packs easily.
- Gluten-free household? Use gluten-free oats.
- Nut-free household? Just replace the 2 cups (500 mL) nuts with an additional 1 cup (250 mL) seeds and 1 cup (250 mL) oats.

(GF, NF, LS)

PROTEIN-PACKED OATMEAL

I'm always trying to find quick and easy ways to incorporate more protein into my diet, especially in the morning when I wake up starving and craving carbs. This protein-packed oatmeal warms my belly, sticks to my ribs and makes me very happy. One portion contains almost 10 grams (0.35 oz) of protein, due to the eggs. Don't worry. This is not scrambled eggs and oatmeal. The eggs are whisked gradually into the oatmeal at the end of the cooking time and delivers a rich and creamy texture.

MAKES 4 servings
PREP TIME 5 minutes
COOK TIME 10 minutes

1 cup (250 mL) large flaked oats

1½ cups (375 mL) milk of choice

1 tsp (5 mL) ground cinnamon

6 eggs, well beaten

1 tsp (5 mL) Pure Vanilla Extract (see p. 14)

1 Tbsp (15 mL) maple syrup, honey or AA Butter (see p. 22), for garnish

1. Measure oats, milk and cinnamon into a small saucepot. Over medium heat, bring to a boil then reduce to simmer, covered for 5–6 minutes, until oats are tender.
2. In a bowl, whisk eggs. Remove oatmeal from heat and slowly pour in the eggs while stirring the oatmeal. Put oatmeal back over medium heat and, stirring constantly, heat until steaming. Do not boil. After about 2–3 minutes, you will see oatmeal start to thicken quickly.
3. Take oatmeal off heat, stir in vanilla extract and transfer to bowls immediately. Residual heat from the pot may cause eggs to curdle.

PORRIDGE TIPS

- Gluten-free household? Use gluten-free oats.
- Eating only egg whites these days? Separate the yolks from the whites and use the whites of six eggs instead.

(V, GF, NF, LS)

BERRY VANILLA RHUBARB COMPOTE

A simple compote is one of the best ways to capture the taste of seasonal fruit. I get so excited when I see local berries after the long grey winter that I want to buy them all. Making compote has become a great way to justify buying too many berries and also the best way to use up fruit that's just past its prime. Here I have mixed some of my favourite summer flavours and combined them with a pure vanilla bean and warming spices to create a compote that can be served warm or cold, morning, noon and night. Serve for breakfast over pancakes, for an afternoon snack with seeds and yogurt or for dessert overtop a little cake or ice cream.

MAKES 8–10 servings
PREP TIME 5 minutes
COOK TIME 8–10 minutes

- 1 vanilla bean
- 3 cups (750 mL) chopped rhubarb
- ½ cup (125 mL) honey
- 2 Tbsp (30 mL) water
- 1 Tbsp (15 mL) fresh lemon juice
- 1 star anise
- ½ cinnamon stick
- 1 Tbsp (15 mL) fresh grated ginger
- 1½ cups (375 mL) raspberries, blueberries or strawberries
- 1½ cups (375 mL) pitted cherries
- 1–2 Tbsp (15–30 mL) orange flower water or ½ tsp (2 mL) orange oil or zest of half an orange (optional)

1. Split vanilla pod lengthwise with a paring knife and, using the back of your knife, scrape out the seeds from inside. Add scraped seeds and pod into a medium-sized saucepan.
2. Add chopped rhubarb, honey, water, lemon juice, star anise, cinnamon and ginger slices. Put saucepan over medium heat and bring to a boil. Lower heat and simmer for 3–5 minutes, or until rhubarb starts to soften.
3. Stir in berries and cherries and continue to simmer for another 5 minutes, stirring occasionally. Rhubarb and berries will break down. Cherries should remain intact but tender.
4. Remove from heat and stir in the orange flower water, oil or zest (if using). Remove the vanilla pod (and reuse, see Saved My Life p. 14), cinnamon stick and star anise. Serve warm or cold. Store in an airtight container in the fridge for a week, or freeze.

COMPOTE TIP

- Compote is simply whole or chopped fruit cooked with water and sugar to a desired consistency, so you can easily customize this recipe according to whatever fruit is in season.

COOL FACT: ORANGE FLOWER WATER MAY BE EVEN COOLER THAN ORANGE OIL

Orange flower water (or orange blossom water) captures the essence of orange blossoms. It is wonderfully fragrant, almost like a perfume. It can be found in most gourmet food shops and is something I do like to splurge on. A bottle will last me up to year and for any foodie it makes a great gift.

(V, GF, NF, LS)

MY GROUND SEED MIX

This is not a recipe as much as it is an ingredient. Over the years, I somehow got into the habit of grinding up a bunch of seeds, mixing them all together and storing them in my fridge. Ground seeds are easier to digest, which makes for easier nutrient absorption. This way adding extra fibre and nutrients to any meal or recipe is within arm's reach. You have no excuse. It is also way cheaper to buy seeds whole than ground.

My kids jokingly call it birdseed and I always travel with a bag of it in my suitcase. I can add a couple tablespoons over yogurt, mixed in with fresh fruit or on top of oatmeal when I travel. I use it as an ingredient in recipes throughout this book to show you how easy it is to cook with.

MAKES 1½ cups (375 mL)
TOTAL TIME 5 minutes
SPECIAL EQUIPMENT NEEDED grinder or small food processor

- ½ cup (125 mL) flax seeds
- ½ cup (125 mL) raw pumpkin seeds
- ½ cup (125 mL) raw sesame seeds
- ½ cup (125 mL) raw sunflower seeds

1. Grind seeds in batches in a small food processor or spice grinder.
2. Mix the ground seeds together and store in an air-tight container or resealable plastic bag.
3. Use as you wish, such as in my Use-Up-the-Zucchini Oatmeal Chocolate Chip Cookies (see p. 159), My Coffee Shop Berry Muffins (see p. 161) and Ginger, Peach and Wild Blueberry Crisp (see p. 178).

SAVED MY LIFE: A CHEAP COFFEE GRINDER

I bought a $10 coffee grinder years ago that I only use for nuts, seeds and spices. Marked with a black Sharpie that says, "No Coffee!" to prevent coffee oils and flavours from permeating through ground spices, nuts and seeds.

GROUND SEED MIX TIP

- There is nothing worse than a bad seed. Nuts and seeds go rancid fairly quickly so if storing for longer than a month, store in the fridge or freezer.

(V, GF, NF, LS)

"FULLY LOADED" PROTEIN BARS

After a long run or a good workout I need a boost of energy to replenish burnt calories and keep me going for the rest of the day. I've tried the coffee and chocolate route, but we all know how that one ends. The best solution for the mind, body and tastebuds is definitely these protein-packed oat bars. I always throw one or two into my gym bag, purse and car so that I can reboot anytime I need to. Simple to make, convenient to take and absolutely delicious to eat!

MAKES 8–10 bars
PREP TIME 10 minutes
COOLING TIME 1 hour (approx.)
SPECIAL EQUIPMENT NEEDED food processor, 8 × 8 inch (20 × 20 cm) square pan

2 cups (500 mL) pitted Medjool dates (about 24)

2 Tbsp (30 mL) vanilla protein powder of choice

2 Tbsp (30 mL) unsalted nut or seed butter

1 tsp (5 mL) Pure Vanilla Extract (see p. 14)

3 Tbsp (45 mL) coconut oil, melted

Pinch of salt

⅓ cup (80 mL) ground flax seeds

½ cup (125 mL) unsweetened flaked coconut

2 cups (500 mL) rolled oats

½ cup (125 mL) hemp seeds

1. Grease a baking pan with coconut oil or line with parchment paper.
2. In a food processor, combine pitted dates, protein powder, nut butter, vanilla, melted coconut oil and salt. Pulse and process to form a thick paste, scraping down the sides when necessary.
3. In a large bowl, stir together all remaining dry ingredients.
4. Add date paste to dry ingredients and knead with hands until everything is incorporated.
5. Transfer to a pan and, using fingertips or the back of a spoon, press to the edges to form a single, even layer.
6. Cover with plastic wrap and chill in the fridge to set, approximately 1 hour.
7. Cut into squares or bars.

SAVED MY LIFE: HAVING PROTEIN POWDER IN MY PANTRY

I like the convenience of protein powder. It really is the quickest way to absorb protein without having to sit and eat six eggs. For this reason, I always keep a good-quality brand stocked in my pantry. I have no interest in building mass and am not partial to the hype of fun flavours or fancy packaging, so I look for the most natural low carb, low fat and high protein (0.6–1 oz/20–30 g serving) brands.

PROTEIN BAR TIP

- Skip the baking pan and roll bars into walnut-sized fancy energy balls or truffles. Hipster coffee shops sell these for a small fortune.

(GF, NF, LS)

PERFECTED PANCAKE RECIPE

Yes, I have probably made pancakes over 100 times. I make them almost every weekend and I am always changing them up. From time to time I try hiding things in the batter—hopefully without my kids noticing, saying "ew" or calling them "too healthy."

They say if you do something 100 times you can get it perfect. Well, this recipe is my all-time favourite. These pancakes are fluffy, buttery and nutty with faint specks of buckwheat.

When it comes to pancakes, you have a lot of room to move around and experiment. It is the fluffiness and the consistency of the batter you have to get right. Start with this recipe and then take it from there. See Pancake Tips (next page) for variations.

MAKES 16–18 small to medium-sized pancakes
PREP TIME 10 minutes
COOK TIME 20 minutes

- 6 Tbsp (90 mL) butter, melted and cooled
- 1¾ cups (435 mL) all-purpose flour
- ¼ cup (60 mL) buckwheat flour
- Pinch of salt
- 4 tsp (20 mL) baking powder
- 4 eggs, at room temperature
- 1½ cups (375 mL) whole milk, at room temperature
- 1 Tbsp (15 mL) apple cider vinegar
- 2 Tbsp (30 mL) honey or maple syrup or 3 drops liquid stevia
- 1 Tbsp (15 mL) Pure Vanilla Extract (see p. 14)

1. In a small saucepan, melt butter over medium-low heat. Set aside to cool.
2. Mix all dry ingredients together in a large bowl.
3. Combine all wet ingredients together in a separate bowl, mixing well to incorporate the eggs. Add in the cooled butter last.
4. Make a well in the centre of your dry ingredients. Pour wet into dry and whisk until combined. Small lumps are completely normal. Adjust your consistency if needed by adding a little more milk. It should be the consistency of a thick batter that just slowly pours off a ladle, not plops.
5. Allow batter to rest 5–10 minutes on a countertop to let gluten relax. You should start to see bubbles percolating. This is good.
6. Preheat a large non-stick skillet over medium heat. Add just enough butter (or coconut oil) to thinly coat the pan and start ladling pancakes to your desired size or shape. I can usually fit 4 pancakes in at a time. When bubbles begin to form on the surface they are ready to flip over. Continue to cook for another minute or so until the batter is cooked though.
7. Serve immediately or let cool on a wire rack and store in an airtight container for up to 2 days. These are also freezer friendly.

SAVED MY LIFE: FREEZING PANCAKES

If I have a busy few weeks of early mornings I will make a double batch, stack with a little piece of parchment or wax paper between each pancake and store in freezer-safe bags. Let the kids pop them in the toaster on a low setting on busy mornings.

PANCAKE TIPS

- For decadent buttermilk pancakes, substitute in buttermilk and omit vinegar.
- For a dairy-free version, use 1½ cups (375 mL) unsweetened milk alternative, like almond, coconut, rice or soy milk.
- To upgrade the texture and flavour, reduce to ¾ cup (185 mL) milk and add ¾ cup (185 mL) ricotta.
- If you're craving pumpkin pie flavours reduce to 1 cup (250 mL) milk and add ½ cup (125 mL) pumpkin purée.
- See how I have used apple cider vinegar in this recipe? Just like buttermilk, the apple cider vinegar, being an acid, aids in the leavening process, making a fluffier pancake. You can use lemon juice as well; my kids, of course, complain of the lemony taste.

COOL FACT: HOW TO GET EGGS TO ROOM TEMPERATURE FAST

To get eggs to room temperature quickly, place them in a bowl of warm water for a few minutes.

(GF, LS, NF)

OMELETTE WITH SPROUTS AND PESTO

I started buying and trying all these different spouts and microgreens for food styling, mostly, since they look so darn pretty in pictures. They also make a awesome salad. I will admit, however, they are sometimes not the easiest to eat, unless they are stuffed in something like a sandwich or a wrap . . . or an omelette! The heat of the omelette gently wilts the sprouts as they get blanketed in pesto. Also, if you've never had pesto with your eggs you don't know what you're missing.

MAKES 1 omelette
TOTAL TIME 10–15 minutes
SPECIAL EQUIPMENT NEEDED good 8-inch (20 cm) non-stick skillet

2–3 eggs (I like a 2-egg omelette, some like 3)

Salt to taste

Pepper to taste

1 Tbsp (5 mL) avocado oil, butter or olive oil

2 Tbsp (30 mL) pesto (for homemade see p. 16)

Handful (about ¾ cup/ 185 mL) sprouts or microgreens of choice (like peas shoots, sunflower, broccoli or radish sprouts)

½ cup (125 mL) grated cheese of choice (Gruyere is especially good here; optional)

1. Using a fork, whisk eggs, salt and pepper in a medium bowl until no streaks remain.
2. Add oil (or butter) to a skillet and melt over medium heat. Let it coat the bottom of the pan and let the pan get good and hot.
3. Pour eggs into a pan and, using a rubber spatula, stir the eggs quickly in a figure-eight pattern while moving the skillet in a circular motion. Cooked bits on the side of pan can be scraped down easily while uncooked eggs takes their place.
4. As soon as the eggs begin to set, about 2 minutes, shake the skillet to settle any uncooked egg. The eggs should be cooked through on the bottom but still runny on top. Lift an edge of the omelette to check that it's holding together.
5. Add your dollops of pesto, handful of sprouts and cheese, if using, over one half of the omelette.
6. Tip the skillet and use your spatula to gently fold the undressed half overtop the filled half.
7. Slide omelette onto a plate and eat immediately.

SAVED MY LIFE: AVOCADO OIL

A heart-healthy oil that can take the heat of a 500°F (260°C) pan? Yes please! Avocado oil is one of my new favourite oils to have on hand.

COOL FACT: WHAT IS THE DIFFERENCE BETWEEN SPROUTS AND MICROGREENS?

Microgreens are a lot like sprouts and the two can often be used interchangeably, but there are a few main differences. Sprouts are grown in water, and they grow in about a week. Microgreens, on the other hand, are grown in soil and can take up to a few weeks to grow. The seed of the sprout is eaten, whereas with microgreens the seed is not eaten, just the plant's first set of leaves. Sprouts are also known to have more crunch than microgreens, depending on variety, while microgreens are said to have more nutritional value as well as more flavour.

(NF, LS)

EGGS ON AVOCADO TOAST

Who knew eggs on toast would be even better with smashed up avocado? A simple recipe where three great things—fluffy eggs, luscious ripe avocado and buttered toasty bread—all come together to create something truly mouthwatering. I swear I would be quite happy eating this everyday.

MAKES 4 servings
PREP TIME 5 minutes
COOK TIME 10 minutes
SPECIAL EQUIPMENT NEEDED non-stick sauté pan

½ Tbsp (7 mL) olive oil

½ Tbsp (7 mL) butter + extra for the toast

4 eggs

Salt to taste

Pepper to taste

4 slices of sourdough

2 avocados

2 Tbsp (30 mL) thinly sliced green onions or chives (optional)

1. Preheat a medium-sized non-stick sauté pan over medium heat. Add olive oil and butter.
2. In a bowl, whisk eggs well until no streaks remain and season with salt and pepper. When butter is melted and foamy, pour in the eggs to coat bottom of pan. As eggs begin to set around the edges, pull to one side of the pan with a heatproof spatula, creating large soft curds. Tilt the pan so that the uncooked eggs move to the other side to set. Continue doing this until all the eggs are set.
3. Toast the bread, and spread each slice with a nice layer of butter.
4. Cut avocados in half, scoop out the flesh into a bowl and smash it up with a fork. Season with salt and pepper.
5. Top buttered toast with smashed avocado and a portion of scrambled eggs. Season with more salt and pepper if needed, and garnish with green onions or chives. Eat with a knife and fork.

SAVED MY LIFE: HAVING ONE GOOD NON-STICK SAUTÉ PAN

I'm not going to get into whether or not non-stick pans are bad for you. I love my non-stick pan. I have a good one and I use it for eggs mostly. I only have two things to say about them: even if it says you can use metal utensils on them, don't, and do not heat a non-stick pan past 500°F (260°C).

(V, GF, NF, LS)

CARROT ZUCCHINI CHIA BISCUITS

I have tried, very unsuccessfully so far, to cut out sugar. I can cut down, yes, but go cold turkey? No way. I admire those out there who have successfully managed to weed sugar out of their diets. This recipe came into fruition when I was looking for an easy biscuit with very little sugar but lots of flavour and nutrients. Here you have carrots, zucchini, banana and coconut folded into a moist, dense and very filling biscuit. These muffins are vegan, but are also wonderful warm and smothered in butter.

MAKES 12 biscuits
PREP TIME 15 minutes
COOK TIME 20 minutes
SPECIAL EQUIPMENT NEEDED blender (optional)

- 1 overripe banana
- ½ cup (125 mL) milk of choice, unsweetened
- ⅓ cup (80 mL) coconut oil, melted
- ¼ cup (60 mL) maple syrup
- 2 Tbsp (30 mL) chia seeds
- 2 Tbsp (30 mL) flax seeds, ground
- 2 cups (500 mL) all-purpose flour
- 2 tsp (10 mL) baking powder
- ½ tsp (2 mL) baking soda
- 1 tsp (5 mL) ground cinnamon
- ½ tsp (2 mL) nutmeg
- ½ tsp (2 mL) ground ginger
- Pinch of salt
- 1 cup (250 mL) finely grated carrots
- 1 cup (250 mL) finely grated zucchini
- ½ cup (125 mL) grated unsweetened coconut

1. Preheat oven to 400°F (200°C); grease a muffin tray or use liners.
2. Using a blender, purée banana with milk, coconut oil and maple syrup. Alternately, you can mash the banana by hand, but this way ensures there are no clumps of banana in the biscuits.
3. Transfer this mixture into a large bowl, stir in the chia and flax seeds and set aside for a few minutes.
4. In the meantime, in a separate bowl whisk together the flour, baking powder, baking soda, spices and salt.
5. Grate carrots and zucchini at this time and set aside.
6. Stir dry ingredients into wet ingredients in 2 additions until just combined. Fold in carrots, zucchini and coconut to form a (unusually) thick batter. Portion batter and fill each muffin cup three-quarters full. This batter can also be pressed down and punched out with cookie cutters.
7. Bake for 20 minutes, until golden brown on top and a toothpick in the centre comes out clean. Let rest for 5 minutes, then transfer muffins to a wire rack to cool. Store in an airtight container for up to 3 days. Freezer friendly.

SAVED MY LIFE: HAND-IMMERSION BLENDERS

I went without a blender until very recently. One of the reasons was that I could make smoothies, puréed soup and even simple batters with my hand-immersion blender. Inexpensive, lightweight (perfect for travelling with) and easy to use (typically just one button to press), it is a no-nonsense piece of kitchen equipment. Perfect for kids and teens (think dormitories), plus they take up way less space than any countertop blender.

(NF, LS)

MORNING GLORY MUFFINS

Muffins, over the years, have gotten a bad reputation. The really good ones, let's be honest, are little cakes, not muffins, with a lot of sugar and fat.

I have always loved a good morning glory muffin, but I needed to create a recipe for them that used less sugar and fat. What I created was a muffin with a minimal combination of maple syrup and cane sugar, which allowed the true sweetness of carrot, pineapple and apple to shine through. I have also packed this recipe full of spices, ground seeds and coconut (oil and shredded) so the muffins are super dense and moist. These, for sure, will help you get out of bed in the morning.

MAKES 16–18 muffins
PREP TIME 20 minutes
BAKE TIME 20–25 minutes

- 1 cup (250 mL) spelt flour
- 1 cup (250 mL) unbleached all-purpose flour
- 1 tsp (5 mL) baking powder
- 1 tsp (5 mL) baking soda
- 3 Tbsp (45 mL) My Ground Seed Mix (see p. 44; optional)
- 1 tsp (5 mL) ground cinnamon
- ½ tsp (2 mL) ground ginger
- ⅛ tsp (0.5 mL) ground cloves
- Pinch of salt
- 2 eggs
- ½ cup (125 mL) plain yogurt
- ½ cup (125 mL) melted coconut oil, cooled
- ¾ cup (185 mL) drained crushed pineapple
- ¼ cup (60 mL) reserved pineapple juice or orange juice
- ⅓ cup (80 mL) maple syrup or honey
- ¼ cup (60 mL) cane sugar
- 1 orange, zested
- 1-inch (2.5 cm) piece fresh ginger, grated
- 1 tsp (5 mL) Pure Vanilla Extract (see p. 14)
- 2 cups (500 mL) finely grated carrots
- 1 finely grated apple
- ½ cup (125 mL) unsweetened shredded coconut
- 1 cup (250 mL) white chocolate chips (optional)

1. Preheat oven to 400°F (200°C) and grease a muffin tray with coconut oil or line with muffin liners.
2. In a large bowl, sift together flours with the baking powder, baking soda, seed mix, dry spices and salt.
3. In another large bowl, whisk together the eggs, yogurt, coconut oil, pineapple, juice, maple syrup, sugar, orange zest, grated ginger and vanilla.
4. Add dry ingredients to wet and stir until just combined.
5. Fold in the grated carrots, apple, coconut and white chocolate, if using.
6. Divide batter evenly into muffin trays, filling up liners three-quarters full.
7. Bake for 20–25 minutes or until a toothpick comes out clean. Let the muffins sit 5 minutes in the tray before moving to a cooling rack.

SAVED MY LIFE: DISHERS OR PORTIONERS

These look like ice cream scoops and come in a variety of sizes, available either online or in kitchen and restaurant supply stores. If you have an ice cream scoop, great, that can be used too! Use it to divide batter evenly into muffin trays. I have a few different-sized dishers at home and use them constantly for consistency and ease of use.

MUFFIN TIPS

- Muffins are best eaten within the first 2 days. After that, freeze them.
- I went without buying a cooling rack for years, so when I made muffins I would simply turn them on their sides in the muffin tray so the air could circulate under them.

PACKED LUNCHES

I hate packing school lunches. There, I said it.

For anyone with school-age children like me, the daily packing of lunches occupies at least three-quarters of the year—for many years to come.

Every morning I am searching for containers. After all these years, my children still can't seem to remember to unpack their lunches, or at the very least bring their lunch bags home. How many times have I combed the school hallways looking for lost lunch bags and Thermoses? Where do they go? How much money have I spent?

My kids went from daycare, where they were getting a nice leisurely hot lunch every day, to being rushed in and out of a hot gymnasium full of screaming kids. In the winter, they would have to dress in or take all their snow gear with them to the lunchroom. You can imagine my sadness after finding my kids' lunches completely uneaten the first few weeks of elementary school. They just didn't have time to eat.

I don't know how many parents ask me for ideas on what to pack their kids for lunch. I really hope this chapter helps. It was written to provide you ideas, inspiration and, most of all, peace of mind. You need to know I feel your pain—it is not easy. But there will come a time when your children will be all grown up. They will be cooking for themselves and making their own lunches.

A FEW MORE NOTES ON PACKING LUNCHES

- I have labelled all of our containers over the years. When misplaced, this has never facilitated their return.
- Having specific containers for each child makes them accountable for their own containers when they go missing. Colour coordinate or something, then they can't blame each other.
- As much as I love the idea of having one lunch container that has a compartment for everything, my kids were not fans. Every time they went to get a snack for recess they had to open the big container up, sometimes with part of their lunch falling out. They also didn't like other kids seeing their lunch. I guess with so many uncoordinated kids bumping into each other in the hallways it's too chaotic. So a few separate containers for lunch and a snack is the "preferred" choice for school-age children. However, then there are more missing containers as months go by. There is no win-win situation here.
- Appetizers for lunch! On nights when I am dragging my heels, dinner typically turns out to be a snack plate and it is always a hit. I get the biggest platter we have and load it up with different crackers, cheeses, salamis, pickles, dips, jellies, raw veggies, nuts, dried and sliced fruit—whatever I have kicking around. This dining experience has inspired many a school lunch. My kids couldn't be happier with a few crackers, slices of cheese, grapes and raw veggies. Think kids' charcuterie! Fruits, veggies, a seed snack mix, a carb, a protein, something salty and something sweet.
- Get the school involved in healthier choices. A "litterless lunch" policy in schools helps parents, like me, have an excuse not to buy those prepackaged heavily processed snacks in the grocery store aisles.

PICNIC
SIDE
HAM

LUNCHES BENTO STYLE

Anything with or on top of plain rice is widely accepted by most children. I am going to tell you it's a waste of time to make cat shapes with your child's sandwich. It's adorable, but that is not my life. I am going to tell you that simple is better.

It was when I started eating with my kids at Japanese restaurants and seeing how they loved the bento-style meals that I realized, kids love things compartmentalized. They like variety, a little bit of this and a little bit of that, and the feeling of control. A little rice, some cucumber, some form of protein, fruit and a healthy snack make for a fantastic school lunch. However, make sure none of these things touch each other, like cut fruit alongside a sandwich in the same container, heaven forbid.

Here are three ideas, along with a recipe for sushi rice I know your kids will love.

(GF, NF, LS)

RICE WITH STUFF ON TOP (CHIRASHI-ZUSHI)

MAKES 2–3 servings
TOTAL TIME 5–10 minutes

Sushi Rice (see p. 61)

Optional toppings (sushi grade seafood; leftover cooked chicken, pork, beef or fish; hard-boiled eggs; fried eggs; canned flaked tuna; leftover steamed veggies; raw veggies; smoked salmon; avocado; etc.)

2–3 green onions, thinly sliced

2 Tbsp (30 mL) sesame seeds

Soy sauce to taste (or tamari, for a gluten-free option)

1. Divide rice into 2–3 servings depending on size of the belly you are feeding.
2. Place topping(s) of choice on top of the rice.
3. Sprinkle green onions, sesame seeds and soy sauce overtop to taste. Serve cold.

LUNCHES BENTO STYLE CONTINUED . . .

(GF, NF, LS)

SPICY TUNA RICE TRIANGLES (ONIGIRI)

MAKES 4 rice balls or triangles
TOTAL TIME 15 minutes
SPECIAL EQUIPMENT NEEDED triangle onigiri mould (original)

- 1 can tuna, drained
- 2–3 Tbsp (30–45 mL) One-Minute Mayo (see p. 30)
- 1 tsp (5 mL) hot sauce or sriracha to taste
- Salt to taste
- 2 cups (500 mL) Sushi Rice (see p. 61)
- 4 sheets nori (seaweed sheets)

1. In a bowl, mix together the tuna, mayo, hot sauce and salt, adjusting to taste.
2. Wet hands and form rice into balls or triangles, using ½ cup (125 mL) rice for each. Here is where the triangle onigiri moulds (found online or at Japanese markets) come in handy. For balls, create a divot with your thumb, place 1 Tbsp (15 mL) tuna mix inside and cover with rice. For triangles, fill up half the mould with rice, place tuna in the centre and fill with the other half of the rice. Press out of mould to have a perfect triangle onigiri.
3. Wrap well in plastic wrap. Can be made the night before. Cut nori to fit the width of the ball or triangle and pack with lunch to wrap rice ball or triangle before eating.

(GF, NF, LS)

CRAB AND CUCUMBER SUSHI (MAKI)

MAKES 6 rolls
TOTAL TIME 15 minutes
SPECIAL EQUIPMENT NEEDED sushi mat

- Sushi Rice (see p. 61)
- 2 sheets nori (seaweed wraps), cut to 7 × 4 inches (19 × 10 cm)
- ⅓ cucumber, seeded and julienned into 4-inch (10 cm) lengths
- 8 crab sticks
- Wasabi (optional)
- Pickled ginger (optional)
- Soy sauce to taste (or tamari, for a gluten-free option)

1. Divide cooked rice into 6 equal portions.
2. Place nori, shiny side down, on a sushi mat. Place portioned rice on nori with damp hands (rice is very sticky) and, using fingers, evenly place rice to cover three-quarters of the nori closest to you, leaving about a 1-inch (2.5 cm) gap at the top.
3. Place cucumber and crab strips horizontally across the middle of the rice.
4. Picking up the part of the sushi mat closest to you, start rolling rice and nori over the filling, pressing gently and using the mat to complete the roll. Use the mat to seal, press and form.
5. Use a sharp moist knife to cut into portions; you should get 8 pieces per roll. Serve with wasabi, pickled ginger and soy sauce.

(V, GF, NF, LS)

SUSHI RICE

MAKES about 3 cups (750 mL)
TOTAL TIME 30–40 minutes
SPECIAL EQUIPMENT NEEDED mesh sieve, onigiri triangle mould (optional), lunch containers

1 cup (250 mL) sushi rice, rinsed well with water

1¼ cups (310 mL) water

2 inch (5 cm) strip kombu (dried kelp; optional)

2–3 Tbsp (45 mL) sushi vinegar (see Sushi Rice Tips below to easily make your own)

1. Place rice in a mesh sieve and rinse with water thoroughly. Drain well. If time allows, soak rice in a bowl of water 30–60 minutes, then rinse this soaking water off and drain well.
2. In a medium pot add rice, water and kombu, Bring to a boil over medium heat. Once the rice boils, remove kombu, cover and reduce to a low simmer for 10–15 minutes, or according to package instructions. No peeking! Resist the temptation to lift the lid.
3. Remove from heat and let sit 10 minutes with the lid on, or covered with a tea towel.
4. Remove lid and spoon rice out into a bowl. Run a wooden spoon or spatula through the rice, cutting into it from side to side, then top to bottom. Add sushi vinegar a little at a time, tasting as you go.
5. Eat as is or let come to room temperature if forming into sushi. Make sure to use damp hands since this rice is very sticky.

SUSHI RICE TIPS

- To make your own sushi vinegar mix together 3 Tbsp (45 mL) rice vinegar, ½ tsp (2 mL) salt and ¾ Tbsp (11 mL) sugar or honey.
- Wooden bowls are better for cooling sushi rice since they absorb moisture and help prevent rice from getting soggy.

THERMOS LUNCHES

Leftovers do make the best lunches. Reheated chili, take-out Chinese, curry stews, soups and simple pastas (the all-around winner for kids) keep very well in a thermos.

We sometimes forget that a thermos is also meant for cold foods. Think cold grain, bean or pasta salads. Below I have added recipes that will seamlessly fit into your lunches, but think also of the next community picnic or family barbecue. Other examples of really great leftover Thermos lunch recipes are all throughout this cookbook: try my Halloween Soup (see p. 79) or Pot of Chili (see p. 84) recipes.

I hear complaints from many parents about getting the temperature of the food right in a Thermos. Some thermoses keep soup so hot that by the time kids are getting corralled outside to play it hasn't cooled down enough to eat. Or you might have a sucky thermos, providing lukewarm edibles. One trick I have learned to keep a thermos hot until lunch is to fill it with boiling water while reheating the food. Then, dump the water and put in the hot food. As for the soup being "too hot," just don't put boiling soup in a thermos. I get the soup to the temperature I think will be ok for my kids then store it. Ask your kids what the temperature of their lunch was like and adjust from there. Oh, and buy a good thermos and hope it comes home at the end of the day.

(GF, NF, LS)

PASTA WITH BUTTER, NO SAUCE

MAKES 2 servings
TOTAL TIME 15 minutes

- 6 oz (175 g) uncooked pasta of choice
- 2 Tbsp (30 mL) butter
- 2 Tbsp (30 mL) extra virgin olive oil
- 1 clove garlic, minced or puréed
- ½ tsp (2 mL) chili flakes (optional)
- Salt to taste
- Pepper to taste
- 1 Tbsp (15 mL) chopped fresh parsley or basil (optional)
- Grated Parmesan cheese to taste (optional)

1. Cook pasta in a pot of generously salted boiling water according to the time on the package.
2. While pasta is cooking, heat a sauté pan over medium heat and melt butter with the olive oil. Turn down heat to medium-low and add in garlic to soften, about 3–5 minutes, making sure it doesn't burn. If adding a little spice, add chili flakes with the garlic. Turn heat to low if necessary.
3. Once pasta is cooked, drain and toss in the sauté pan with the garlicky goodness. Add salt, pepper and more oil or butter to taste. Stir in chopped herbs and/or Parmesan cheese if you like.

SAVED MY LIFE: LEFTOVER COOKED PASTA

Leftover cooked pasta stores very well in the fridge, so typically whenever I make a pasta dish I cook extra, toss with a little olive oil to prevent sticking and store in a sealed container in the fridge. This way the kids have something they can easily take out and reheat in a pan with a little sauce, or we can tie it into a pasta salad or a dinner idea the next evening.

PASTA TIPS

- I always measure my pasta by eye, which is not necessarily the best way to measure out pasta for portions. Dry pasta generally doubles in size and weight when cooked. Typically you want 2 oz (60 g) pasta per person for a side, or 3 oz (90 g) for a main.
- Pasta is best measured by weight since pasta comes in so many different sizes and shapes.

(V, GF, NF, LS)

KID-FRIENDLY QUINOA TABBOULEH SALAD

MAKES 4 servings
TOTAL TIME 15 minutes

½ cup (125 mL) uncooked quinoa (or 1½ cups/375 mL leftover cooked quinoa)

2 Tbsp (30 mL) extra virgin olive oil

2 Tbsp (30 mL) lemon juice (or to taste)

⅛ tsp (0.5 mL) ground allspice

Salt to taste

Pepper to taste

2 green onions, finely sliced

½ red, orange or yellow pepper, diced into small pieces

½ cup (125 mL) grape or cherry tomatoes, cut in half or quartered

1 cup (250 mL) cucumber, seeded and diced into small pieces

½ cup (125 mL) finely chopped curly parsley

1. Prepare quinoa according to the instructions on the package (or use leftover quinoa).
2. Whisk together a simple vinaigrette in a small bowl with olive oil, lemon juice, allspice, salt and pepper.
3. In a large bowl, combine all remaining ingredients. Gently fold in the cooled quinoa. Pour over vinaigrette, toss, taste and adjust seasoning.

SAVED MY LIFE: LEFTOVER QUINOA

Sometimes if I am making quinoa for a recipe I purposefully make extra to have leftovers for a quick lunch or dinner later in the week. If you like quinoa, I strongly suggest doing the same. It can be eaten morning, noon and night.

TABBOULEH TIP

- This is one of the very few recipes where I recommend using curly parsley. It makes a fluffier salad.

(GF, NF, LS)

CRUNCHY CHOPPED SALAD

MAKES 4–6 servings
COOK TIME 20 minutes

1 cup (250 mL) small broccoli florets

1 cup (250 mL) small cauliflower florets

1 large carrot, peeled and chopped

2 celery stalks, chopped

1 red pepper, cubed

4–5 radishes, diced

½ cup (125 mL) diced fennel bulb

¼ lb (125 g) halloumi cheese, cut into small cubes

1 Tbsp (15 mL) chopped fennel fronds

1 Tbsp (15 mL) chopped fresh dill

GREEK-STYLE DRESSING

½ garlic clove, minced or puréed

1 tsp (5 mL) dried oregano (Greek or mountain oregano is best)

¼ cup (60 mL) fresh lemon juice

1 tsp (5 mL) salt

½ cup (125 mL) extra virgin olive oil

Pepper to taste

1. Add all salad ingredients into a large bowl.
2. Put all ingredients for the dressing into a jar with a lid. Shake violently. Pour over salad and toss.
3. Store in an airtight container for up to 3 days.

SAVED MY LIFE: WILT-FREE VEGETABLES

Any salad I make the kids for lunch has to be wilt-free. It's hard enough convincing my kids to have lettuce in their sandwiches let alone hope they will eat a salad. Raw vegetables that stay crunchy are your only hope. I have tried sending leafy salads along with the dressing in a cute little "leak-proof" container. It either doesn't get eaten or the lunch bags come home coated in oil. Realistically, my kids get 20 minutes to eat their lunch in school. That's if they are actually spending that time eating. They don't want to screw around with dressing a salad when they want to play.

COOL FACT: WHAT THE HELL ARE FENNEL FRONDS?

The feathery dill like fronds attached to the stalks of your fennel bulb, of course.

SMOOTHIES FOR LUNCH

Most kids like smoothies, but you may not think of them as something to pack with your child for lunch, just like I never would have thought to send my daughter off to school with tea until recently (bringing cool-flavoured teas to school to sip on throughout the day has somehow become a thing for girls age 10 and up). Seriously, smoothies are really great, especially if your child is at that age where they have wiggly teeth and it just hurts too much to chew.

If you have a beverage bottle that keeps drinks cold, a smoothie is also the easiest way to send a whole bunch of fruit and/or veggies to school with them. They will probably sip a smoothie before peeling that knocked-around bruised banana.

(V, GF, NF, LS)

THE CLASSIC WITH A TWIST

MAKES 2 cups (500 mL)
TOTAL TIME 5 minutes
SPECIAL EQUIPMENT NEEDED a blender

- ¾ cup (185 mL) milk of choice
- ¼ cup (60 mL) buttermilk, plain yogurt or kefir
- 1 banana
- ½ cup (125 mL) frozen strawberries
- ½ cup (125 mL) frozen mango

1. Fill a blender with milk and buttermilk (or yogurt).
2. Add in remaining ingredients and blend 1–3 minutes depending on the brand of blender.
3. Best to drink right away, but will keep up to 2 days sealed well in the fridge.

(V, GF, NF, LS)

BLUEBERRY FIELDS

MAKES 2 cups (500 mL)
TOTAL TIME 5 minutes
SPECIAL EQUIPMENT NEEDED a blender

- 1 cup (250 mL) milk of choice or yogurt
- 1 banana
- ½ cup (125 mL) blueberries
- 1 cup (250 mL) spinach
- Pinch of cinnamon
- Pinch of nutmeg

1. Fill a blender with milk and/or yogurt.
2. Add in remaining ingredients and blend 1–3 minutes depending on the brand of blender.
3. Best to drink right away, but will keep up to 2 days sealed well in the fridge.

SMOOTHIES FOR LUNCH CONTINUED . . .

(V, GF, NF, LS)

MY HONEST GREEN SMOOTHIE

MAKES about 3 cups (750 mL)
TOTAL TIME 5 minutes
SPECIAL EQUIPMENT NEEDED a blender

2½ cups (500 mL) very cold water, coconut water or a combination of both

1 lemon, juiced

1-inch (2.5 cm) piece ginger, peeled and roughly chopped

1 green apple, skin on, chopped

4 inch (8–10 cm) piece cucumber, chopped

½ banana

2 cups (500 mL) packed kale, spinach or chard (or any combination of)

½ cup (125 mL) packed parsley

2 Tbsp (30 mL) unflavoured protein powder of choice (optional)

1–2 Tbsp (15–30 mL) hemp hearts or ground flax seed (optional)

1. Fill a blender with the water (or coconut water) and lemon juice.
2. Add in remaining ingredients starting with the denser ones, like the ginger and apple. Blend until you have a smoothie-like consistency, 1–3 minutes depending on the brand of blender.
3. Best to drink right away, but keeps up to 24 hours sealed well in the fridge.

SAVED MY LIFE: GREEN SMOOTHIES

As parents, we tend to take care of everyone else first. We get what's left over. Making these smoothies on a regular basis is my way of being good to myself. Making sure I get what I need. If I am carrying a heavy workload, I will make one before bed and grab it as I head out the door. They are cleansing, energizing and healing. Green smoothies have honestly changed my life.

SMOOTHIE TIPS

- Greens that are high in iron, like spinach, are absorbed more easily by your stomach when eaten with an acid like lemon juice or apple cider vinegar.
- I went without a quality blender for a very long time. Everyone I knew had one, but I always came up with some excuse not to splurge. Then I got a good one and it changed my life. This is not some plug to go out and spend a fortune on a blender, but I am saying I use my blender everyday—it has made my life easier and I am healthier for it.

SANDWICHES THAT ACTUALLY GET EATEN

I know this may be hard for you to hear, but those lunches you made may be getting thrown away. When researching sandwiches for this section I very seriously interrogated my son and all his teenage friends. What was their favourite packed lunch? They all said the same thing: pack them money. I was told that if they have money, then they buy something they actually eat. Great.

Well, we all know that this is not a practical, economical or even a remotely healthy solution. I allow my kids one day a week when they can eat out for lunch. So what does that mean? It means that I have to accept that when I pack them a lunch, some of the time, it's not all getting eaten. How many times have you opened that lunch bag to find that precious organic roast chicken sandwich on sourdough without a bite taken out of it? Sometimes packing those lunches is really more for us than them.

Out of all the sandwiches I have made over the years, my kids tell me these are their top three they actually eat. Also, I know, a wrap is not technically a sandwich, but I included one here because kids do like the portability of wraps and it adds a little variety.

(NF, LS)

CLASSIC CHICKEN CAESAR WRAP

MAKES 2 wraps
TOTAL TIME 10 minutes

1 cup (250 mL) cubed left-over cooked chicken or turkey

1½ cups (375 mL) chopped romaine hearts

½ cup (125 mL) diced cucumber

¼ cup (60 mL) croutons (optional)

¼ cup (60 mL) grated Parmesan cheese

⅓ cup (80 mL) Caesar salad dressing (or to taste; for homemade see p. 77)

Salt to taste

Pepper to taste

2 large tortilla wraps

1. In a large bowl, combine the chicken, romaine, cucumber, croutons, Parmesan cheese, salad dressing, salt and pepper. Toss to dress salad.
2. Divide salad between wraps and roll like a burrito.

SAVED MY LIFE: THOSE PREMADE SALAD KITS

I can't believe I am actually saying this after all the years of shunning premade salad kits, but being a single mother with a two kids—one now a teenager—means our schedules are always changing. There is the odd day when I am not home to make lunch or dinner and they have to fend for themselves. If I buy a couple of salad kits, kids can easily throw and mix them in a bowl to eat. Plus, I don't come home with the kitchen looking like a disaster. In a pinch, a premade chicken Caesar salad kit also makes for a super-easy chicken Caesar wrap in the morning.

WRAP TIPS

- Too much dressing makes a soggy wrap. Too much filling means it may fall apart.
- If the wrap feels a little dried out or is cracking, warm it for a few seconds over medium heat in a sauté pan. It will soften up, making it bendier.
- I thought it would be fun to send the kids to school with coloured red and green wraps around the holidays. Nope, they were mortified.

SANDWICHES THAT ACTUALLY GET EATEN CONTINUED . . .

(NF, LS)

SOPHIA'S TUNA SALAD SANDWICH

MAKES 2 sandwiches
TOTAL TIME 10 minutes

- One ⅓-lb (170 g) can tuna, drained
- ¼ cup (60 mL) finely diced shallot
- ¼ cup (60 mL) finely diced celery
- ¼ cup (60 mL) finely diced red pepper
- ¼ cup (60 mL) finely diced pickles
- 1 Tbsp (15 mL) olive oil
- 1 tsp (5 mL) lemon juice
- 1–2 Tbsp (15–30 mL) One-Minute Mayo (see p. 30)
- Salt to taste
- Pepper to taste
- 4 slices grainy bread that your kids will actually eat

1. In a bowl, mix together all ingredients (except the bread) until combined.
2. Divide the tuna salad and, using a spoon, place between 2 slices of bread. Cut in half and place in a container with a small freezer pack to keep cool until lunch.

SAVED MY LIFE: STAINLESS STEEL LUNCH CONTAINERS

Stainless steel lunch containers really do last. I have had the same three for years now. I don't know how they haven't gone missing yet. Knock on wood.

TUNA TIPS

- Canned water-packed light tuna, specifically skipjack, is your best choice. It is lower in mercury and higher in omega-3s.
- Look for cans of tuna that are sustainably caught the old way, with labels saying line-and-pole caught.

(NF, LS)

OZ'S B.F. GRILLED CHEESE BAGEL

MAKES 2 sandwiches
PREP TIME 5 minutes
COOK TIME 5 minutes
SPECIAL EQUIPMENT NEEDED grill press (optional)

- 2 bagels (preferably "everything" bagels), cut in half
- 2 Tbsp (30 mL) butter
- 1 cup (250 mL) grated cheddar cheese or 4 slices
- 2 slices black forest ham
- Pepper to taste

1. Preheat a sauté pan over medium heat.
2. Butter outer slices of bagels. Place one half of each bagel, buttered sides down, in the pan, and layer with cheese, ham, more cheese and pepper to taste. Top with the other halves and, if you have one, place a grill press on top of the sandwich.
3. Let toast for about 2–3 minutes per side until cheese is fully melted and oozing through the hole in the middle and both sides of the bagel are nicely toasted. Cut into quarters to fit inside a Thermos.

SAVED MY LIFE: MY GRILL PRESS

Move over panini press, you take up too much space anyway. Thank you to whoever bought me that small grill press years ago. We use it all the time to make some sort of grilled cheesy goodness in the cast-iron fry pan. They are a great investment and fantastic gift idea.

SALADS AND SOUPS

There are times when a really great soup or salad is all you want. I may even say need. Because sometimes you just need your mother's leftover Christmas turkey stew, or your body craves that big bowl of gently tossed greens. Both can eat like a meal or a starter, or they can sit beside one another. Both provide you with the perfect opportunity for getting creative in the kitchen, using up leftovers and clearing out the fridge.

(V, GF, NF, LS)

HEIRLOOM CARROT AND SPICY SAUERKRAUT QUINOA SALAD

Quinoa is the perfect ingredient: it's a complete protein, it's high in fibre and, because it has a fairly neutral nutty flavour, it pairs with almost everything. When it comes to big hearty salads I like to mix up my ingredients so there is a good balance of flavour and texture. In this instance I've added carrots, daikon radish and pumpkin seeds for crunch, basil and dill for a burst of freshness and—for the pièce de résistance—I've added my spicy sauerkraut. Trust me on this one, everyone will be asking you for this recipe after your next potluck.

Serve this salad on its own as a main, or as a side dish for roast pork and chicken. It also works well packed in lunches, or as a make-ahead for your next dinner party.

MAKES 6 servings
PREP TIME 10 minutes
COOK TIME 15 minutes
SPECIAL EQUIPMENT NEEDED fine mesh sieve

½ cup (125 mL) dried quinoa or 1 cup (250 mL) cooked quinoa

1 bunch (about 4–5) heirloom carrots trimmed, peeled and cut into thin ¼ inch (6 mm) coins

2 Tbsp (30 mL) raw apple cider vinegar or fresh lemon juice

¼ cup (60 mL) extra virgin olive oil

1 Tbsp (15 mL) cold-pressed pumpkin or sesame oil

¼ red onion, finely chopped

1 red or orange pepper, finely diced

½ cup (125 mL) cubed daikon radish

2 Tbsp (30 mL) chopped fresh basil

2 Tbsp (30 mL) chopped fresh dill

4–6 Tbsp (90 mL) spicy sauerkraut (for homemade see p. 28)

Salt to taste

Pepper to taste

½ cup (125 mL) raw pumpkin seeds, for garnish

1. To cook quinoa, rinse well in a fine mesh sieve then simmer, covered, in a medium-sized saucepot according to package instructions. Typically ½ cup (125 mL) quinoa needs ¾ cup (185 mL) of salted water and takes 13 minutes to cook.
2. Place carrots in boiling salted water until just tender, about 3 minutes. They should still have a little bite to them. Drain and shock them under cold water to stop the cooking process.
3. In a large bowl, combine all remaining ingredients except salt, pepper and pumpkin seeds. Stir in the cooked quinoa and season with salt and pepper to taste. Sprinkle with raw pumpkin seeds and drizzle extra olive oil if needed.

COOL FACT: PUMPKIN SEED OIL IS SO GOOD

Pumpkin seed oil has an intense nutty taste and a plethora of nutritional benefits. It's perfect for salads, dressings or drizzled on bread. Use as a finishing oil and never for cooking, and make sure you store it in a cool dark place.

(GF, NF, LS)

CHICKEN AND BROCCOLI QUINOA SALAD

There had to be one chicken and broccoli recipe in this cookbook. This dynamic duo is a standard meal combination in many households. Here is my go-to recipe when I have leftover chicken and a head of broccoli kicking around the fridge. It is more of a broccoli recipe than anything since I only call for a cup of cooked chicken, but feel free to add more if you have it. Might as well use it up.

The addition of finely chopped pickles adds zest and crunch, while the sesame seeds and oil offer a slightly Asian feel. I do suggest trying the crispy shallots as a garnish if you want to take it to the next level. This salad I serve warm or cold, so it is particularly good for packed lunches.

MAKES 4–6 servings
PREP TIME 5 minutes
COOK TIME 15 minutes
SPECIAL EQUIPMENT NEEDED fine mesh sieve

1 cup (250 mL) quinoa, rinsed and drained

1 head (about 3 cups/750 mL) broccoli, broken into large florets

1 cup (250 mL) cooked chicken, cubed (leftovers are great)

2 dill pickles, finely chopped

2 Tbsp (30 mL) sesame oil

¼ cup (60 mL) extra virgin olive oil

2 Tbsp (30 mL) fresh lemon juice (or to taste)

Salt to taste

Pepper to taste

¼ cup (60 mL) raw sesame seeds, for garnish

Crispy Shallots and Garlic Chips (see p. 98), for garnish

1. In a medium-sized saucepot, add a pinch of salt to 1½ cups (375 mL) water and bring to a boil. Add quinoa, turn down to simmer, cover and cook for 12 minutes. Remove from heat and keep covered for 5–10 minutes. Fluff with a fork.
2. Blanch broccoli in boiling salted water for 3–4 minutes, until tender crisp. Drain and run under cold water to stop the cooking process. Dice any long stems and break up large florets into smaller ones. Add both to a large bowl.
3. Add in the chopped chicken, pickles and fluffed quinoa.
4. In a small bowl, mix oils with the lemon juice and season with salt and pepper. Toss into the salad.
5. Sprinkle sesame seeds overtop. If desired, serve with garlic chips and/or crunchy shallots.

QUINOA TIPS

- Quinoa, because of its popularity, can be expensive. Buy in bulk to save money and buy fair trade if you can.
- Always rinse your quinoa. It has a bitter outer coating that needs rinsing. Since quinoa are tiny, a fine mesh sieve will come in handy for this.
- Quinoa comes in white, red and black varieties. They vary so slightly in nutritional value that I choose the variety according to what colour I want to cook instead.
- Ever "sprout" your quinoa? Sprouting or germinating grains before cooking increases nutritional value and makes them easier to digest. Rinse quinoa first and place in a large bowl of water overnight. Rinse and drain well before cooking.

(V, GF, NF, LS)

MY SIMPLE SOUTH-OF-FRANCE GREEN BEAN SALAD

I've taken inspiration from the French for this delicate green bean recipe by keeping it simple, because when it comes to vegetables the French don't mess around. The lightly blanched beans remain tender, yet crisp, and the shallot vinaigrette adds a tangy punch without overwhelming the fresh flavour of the beans. This dish can be served at room temperature or cold out of the fridge, which makes it great for both school lunches (my kids LOVE this one) and as a great make-ahead for your next dinner party.

MAKES 4–6 servings
PREP TIME 5 minutes
COOK TIME 5 minutes

3 Tbsp (45 mL) white wine vinegar

3 Tbsp (45 mL) extra virgin olive oil

1 shallot, cut in half and finely sliced

Salt to taste

Pepper to taste

1 lb (450 g) green beans, trimmed

3 Tbsp (45 mL) freshly grated Parmesan or Pecorino Romano, for garnish (optional)

⅓ cup (80 mL) toasted nuts or seeds, for garnish (optional)

1. Make a simple vinaigrette with white wine vinegar and olive oil. Toss in sliced shallots. Season with a good pinch of salt and pepper and set aside; let the shallots mingle in the oil and vinegar.
2. Plunge green beans in boiling salted water for 3 minutes, or until just tender crisp. Plunge into an ice bath or run under cold water to cool and prevent overcooking. Set aside on a clean tea towel to dry off excess moisture.
3. Pour shallot vinaigrette over the cool beans and serve with garnishes if you so please.

(GF, NF, LS)

MEXICAN CHICKEN AND VEGETABLE SOUP

Memories make the best recipes.

A few of our family vacations to Mexico when the kids were babies were to the typical all-inclusives that supposedly make it easier to travel with small kids. I remember sitting in a beachfront café with the kids in Playa del Carmen thoroughly loving this simple homemade chicken soup served with fresh Mexican garnishes. This soup is etched in my memory and I always seem to crave it during the cold winter months. I don't know if it was the soup itself or how it brings back all those amazing (yet slightly traumatizing) warm family vacation memories.

Avocado in soup? I know, it seems weird but trust me. Oh, and don't forget the freshly squeezed lime juice.

MAKES 4 servings
PREP TIME 10 minutes
COOK TIME 5 minutes

½ onion, diced

1 Tbsp (15 mL) olive oil

1 clove garlic, finely chopped

2 medium carrots, small dice

2 celery stalks, diced

Salt to taste

Pepper to taste

1 tsp (5 mL) dried oregano (if you can find Mexican oregano, great)

4 cups (1 L) chicken stock

1 cup (250 mL) shredded cooked chicken

1 cup (250 mL) frozen corn

1 avocado, diced

2 tomatoes, diced

½ cup (125 mL) chopped cilantro

1 jalapeno, finely minced

6 lime wedges

Corn tortilla chips, for serving

1. In a large saucepot over medium heat, sauté onion in olive oil until translucent, about 3 minutes. Add garlic, carrots and celery, season lightly with salt and pepper and continue to sauté until vegetables start to soften, about 5 minutes.
2. Add oregano and stock and simmer until vegetables are tender. Add in chicken and corn to heat through.
3. While the soup is cooking, chop all remaining ingredients and place in a serving bowl (or bowls) to garnish soup at the table.
4. Serve up soup with the garnishes and let people add what they want. You will taste the flavours change as you add a squeeze of lime and spice it up with jalapenos. Serve with a bowl full of corn tortilla chips.

COOL FACT: YOU CAN GRILL AVOCADO

Have you ever grilled an avocado? Try thick slices of avocado thrown on a preheated grill, get some grill marks and serve on a salad or layered on top of your next barbecued burger.

(GF, NF, LS)

BEET GREENS AND KALE SEEDED CAESAR SALAD

I'll be honest, this is a more adult version of a Caesar salad. However, toss this same dressing on romaine lettuce, croutons and bacon and you will have an another instant winner. Come on, we have all been known to make a kid and adult version of the same recipe at dinnertime.

I also have been able to eat this whole salad by myself in one sitting, and you may have more Seeded Caesar Salad Dressing than required for the one salad. Don't worry, any extra dressing will be quickly used up as a dip for raw veggies or spread on tomorrow's sandwich.

The seeds in this recipe make a creamy dressing and take the place of raw egg. Nutritional yeast can be used instead of Parmesan cheese if you are trying to cut the fat as ¼ cup (60 mL) of Parmesan has 64 calories in comparison to nutritional yeast's 5 calories.

MAKES 2 mains or 4 sides
TOTAL TIME 15 minutes
SPECIAL EQUIPMENT NEEDED good blender or small food processor, salad spinner (optional)

1 bunch of kale (leafy greens only), finely chopped

1 bunch of beet greens, washed well, leaves finely chopped

3 beets, peeled and cut into wedges, roasted (optional; see Cool Fact below)

2–4 Tbsp (30–60 mL) nutritional yeast or grated Parmesan cheese, for garnish

2 Tbsp (30 mL) raw sesame or hemp seeds, for garnish

SEEDED CAESAR SALAD DRESSING

2 cloves garlic, smashed and chopped

¼ cup (60 mL) raw sesame or hemp seeds

¼ cup (60 mL) nutritional yeast (see Saved My Life p. 16) or grated Parmesan cheese

¼ cup (60 mL) fresh lemon juice

¼ cup (60 mL) water

¼ cup (60 mL) extra virgin olive oil

4 anchovies

Salt to taste

Pepper to taste

1. Prepare salad greens. Got a salad spinner? Use it. If not, wrap washed leaves in a clean tea towel and gently shake off excess water. Place in a large salad bowl. The drier the leaves the better the dressing will coat the greens. Place greens in the salad bowl.
2. In a blender or small food processor, combine all ingredients for the dressing, except salt and pepper, and blend until you have a thick and creamy dressing. Taste and season with salt and pepper.
3. Pour half the dressing over the greens and massage with your hands until the greens are coated and slightly limp. Taste and add more dressing if needed.
4. Serve with roasted beet wedges (if desired), seeds and a sprinkle more of nutritional yeast or Parmesan cheese.

BEET GREEN TIPS

- When buying beets, buy the ones with the greens attached. These greens, like radish greens (which can be eaten as well), tend to be sandy and will require a good wash. Store washed greens in a plastic bag or container.
- Vegetables like carrots and beets go rubbery quickly if you leave their tops attached. Trim tops before storing. The tops and leaves will suck the moisture out of the roots for themselves.

COOL FACT: PEELS SLIP OFF ROASTED BEETS EASILY

To roast beets, place washed, trimmed, unpeeled beets in a double-layer foil package with 1 Tbsp (15 mL) olive oil drizzled overtop. Seal the package and roast at 425°F (220°C) for 45 minutes to an hour, until fork tender. For more flavour, add a few garlic cloves, sprigs of fresh rosemary or thyme to the package. When the beets are cool their peels will slip off easily.

(GF, LS)

CHICKEN SOUP AU PISTOU

A tablespoon of pesto added to each bowl of this classic French Provençal soup brings plain old chicken soup to a whole other level. It's so easy—a chicken and vegetable soup with pesto, ready in no time at all. You can make the pistou (pesto) while the vegetables are getting tender, or just use store bought. I do suggest having some extra pesto in a serving bowl to pass around at the table. This soup is also especially good for school lunches.

MAKES 6 servings
PREP TIME 10 minutes
COOK TIME 20 minutes

- 2 Tbsp (30 mL) olive oil
- 1 onion, finely chopped
- 3 medium carrots, small dice
- 3 celery stalks, small dice
- 5 sprigs fresh thyme, leaves only
- 2 bay leaves
- 8 cups (2 L) chicken stock
- 1 cup (250 mL) trimmed green beans, cut into ½-inch (1 cm) pieces
- Salt to taste
- Pepper to taste
- 6 Tbsp (90 mL) pesto (for homemade see p. 16)

1. In a large saucepot over medium heat, add the oil and sauté onion to soften, about 3 minutes.
2. Stir in the carrots and celery, season lightly with salt and pepper and continue to cook, stirring occasionally, so vegetables soften slightly, about 4–5 minutes. Do not brown.
3. Add thyme, bay leaves, stock and green beans. Bring soup up to simmer and cook until vegetables are tender, about 10–15 minutes. Taste and season with salt and pepper.
4. While the soup is simmering you can use this time to make pesto, or use store bought.
5. Place 1 Tbsp (15 mL) pesto in the bottom of each serving bowl and ladle soup overtop. Stir pesto into the soup and enjoy.

SAVED MY LIFE: CHOPPING THINGS SMALLER

The smaller it's chopped, the faster it will cook. Therefore, I would rather spend a little extra time properly cutting things into uniform pieces for quicker, even cooking. It also makes for nice presentation, which I am a sucker for.

(GF, NF, LS)

HALLOWEEN SOUP

"This was the soup I served you little ones after the Santa Claus Parade and on Halloween before Trick or Treating," my mother's best friend Kathy Parsons told me when I asked her about it decades later. "Everyone had to have one full bowl before going out. I called it Hamburger Soup (traditionally called Cabbage Soup) because that sounds more appealing to young children. You may remember it as Halloween Soup. I had to triple this recipe sometimes."

Well, Kathy, I made just a few small adjustments to your famous recipe, which is a hit all around my table. I also halved the original recipe for a family of four. I do highly suggest doubling it when feeding a crowd—you need a freezer-friendly meal or something that can be eaten over the course of a few days.

Kathy, I truly admire how you managed to keep us all so well fed through all those years. It was always a treat to visit, and to eat what was hidden in your freezer.

MAKES 4–6 servings
PREP TIME 20 minutes
COOK TIME 30–40 minutes
SPECIAL EQUIPMENT NEEDED large stockpot

- ½ lb (250 g) lean ground beef
- 2 Tbsp (30 mL) olive oil, divided
- 1 onion, diced
- 1 lb (450 g) carrots (about 5–6), peeled and diced
- 4 celery sticks, diced
- ½ small cabbage, cored and chopped
- 1 cup (250 mL) diced potatoes
- 1 green pepper, diced
- Salt to taste
- Pepper to taste
- One 5½-oz (156 mL) can tomato paste
- One 28-oz (796 mL) can whole or chopped tomatoes
- 3 cups (750 mL) beef broth
- 1 tsp (5 mL) paprika
- 1 Tbsp (15 mL) dried parsley
- 1 Tbsp (15 mL) dried oregano
- 1 Tbsp (15 mL) dried savory
- 2 bay leaves

1. In a large stockpot over medium-high heat, brown ground beef with 1 Tbsp (15 mL) olive oil, about 5 minutes. Transfer to a paper towel–lined plate.
2. In the same pot over medium heat, add 1 Tbsp (15 mL) olive oil and cook the onions until translucent, about 3 minutes. Add carrots, celery, cabbage, potatoes and green pepper. Continue to cook for another 5 minutes to soften vegetables slightly. Season with a good pinch of salt and pepper.
3. Add all remaining ingredients, stir, bring to a boil, turn down to simmer and cover for about 30 minutes or until vegetables are tender. If vegetables are not completely covered with beef stock add a little more stock or water.
4. Taste and season with salt and pepper as needed.

SAVED MY LIFE: KEEPING ALL THOSE OLD FAMILY RECIPES

Believe me, it is these recipes that will heal you through the tough times, and people love to share old family recipes. I'm not so good at recording history with photos or videos but I am so glad I did keep my mother's old recipes. Every now and then, when I do visit "back home," the one thing I love taking with me are the recipes that hold the secrets to all my childhood memories.

SOUP TIP

- Keep vegetable cuts, like potatoes, carrots and celery, all the same size so they cook evenly. You don't want the carrots to be mushy and the potatoes still hard.

(V, GF, NF, LS)

PURÉE OF CELERIAC AND LEEK SOUP

Celeriac, aka celery root, is not a particularly common or good-looking vegetable, so it's no surprise they tend to go unnoticed in grocery stores. But this is one underrated root vegetable.

What is celeriac you ask? It is very closely related to celery, but celeriac is only cultivated for its root end instead of its stems and leaves. Its beastly looking, gnarly exterior is usually the size of a rutabaga, and may or may not have its celery like stems attached; it will, for sure, have many traces of dirt and sand in its nooks and crannies. But don't let its appearance fool you—once trimmed of its outer skin you will find a subtly sweet and creamy interior, and something magical happens when you blend it in a silky smooth purée. The smell alone of leeks and onions cooking is a good enough reason to make this soup. Don't forget the splash of apple cider vinegar or white wine at the end. Sometimes a little acidity at the end of a recipe is exactly what was missing.

MAKES 6 servings
PREP TIME 10 minutes
COOK TIME 20 minutes
SPECIAL EQUIPMENT NEEDED blender or food processor or hand-immersion blender

- 2 small or 1 large celeriac (about 2 lb/900 g)
- 2 Tbsp (30 mL) butter
- 2 Tbsp (30 mL) olive oil
- 1 onion, diced
- 2 large or 3 small leeks, white and light green parts only, washed well and thinly sliced
- 2 cloves garlic, smashed and roughly chopped
- 2 bay leaves
- 10 sprigs fresh thyme
- Salt to taste
- Freshly ground white pepper to taste
- 4 cups (1 L) chicken or vegetable stock, divided
- 1–2 Tbsp (30 mL) apple cider vinegar, white wine or white wine vinegar

1. Wash celeriac well and peel skin with a knife, then cut into 1-inch (2.5 cm) cubes. This should yield about 4 cups (1 L), or little over 1 lb (450 g).
2. Preheat a large saucepot or stockpot over medium and melt butter with the oil.
3. Sauté onion and leeks for about 5 minutes until onion is translucent.
4. Stir in the garlic, bay leaves, thyme and celeriac. Season with salt and white pepper.
5. Pour 3 cups (750 mL) stock into the pot, just enough to cover ingredients. Bring to a boil and lower to simmer until celeriac is very tender, about 15–20 minutes.
6. Remove from heat; fish out the bay leaves and thyme stems and discard. Purée in a pot with a hand-immersion blender, or transfer to a food processor or blender for an even smoother, silkier consistency, then return to the pot.
7. Over medium-low heat, adjust consistency of the purée by stirring in additional stock. I usually find it a little too thick at this point so I add the additional 1 cup (250 mL) stock. Taste and season with salt, white pepper and finish with a splash of apple cider vinegar or white wine before serving.

CELERIAC TIPS

- When buying celeriac, make sure to look for a root that is firm and free from any major spots or damage. Since this root is often overlooked, it may have spent too much time in the vegetable aisle and have become rubbery. Avoid these. Also, make sure to allow for a quarter of its weight to be discarded as you trim it of its gnarly exterior.
- If celeriac is bought with celery stems attached, trim before storing. This will help the celeriac store longer, up to 2 weeks in the fridge. Peel celeriac using a knife, not a vegetable peeler, and don't worry about having to peel generously. You want to use only its creamy white interior.
- Bored of plain mashed potatoes? Why not do a 50/50 potato and celeriac mash? Boil and mash celeriac chunks exactly the same as you would potatoes.

(GF, NF, LS)

BARONE KALE CALDO VERDE

Crimson-coloured chorizo-flavoured oil creates the base for this simple Spanish soup, otherwise known as "green" soup. Belly warming in the cold winter months, but light enough that it can be made throughout the year, it's filling without being heavy.

Traditionally made with only water, I have upped the ante with homemade stock. I prefer mild chorizo so I have more control over the heat, adding chili flakes as I go.

Why Barone Caldo Verde? Because the first time I had this soup was when Chef Christina Barone made it one year for us at Christmas. She made it with love and love always makes everything taste better.

MAKES 6 servings
PREP TIME 20 minutes
COOK TIME 25 minutes
SPECIAL EQUIPMENT NEEDED stockpot, blender (or hand-immersion blender) or food processor

¼ cup (60 mL) olive oil, divided

½ lb (250 g) dry-cured Spanish chorizo (mild or hot), cut in half lengthwise then thinly sliced

2 cups (500 mL) diced onion

3 garlic cloves, minced

½ tsp (2 mL) chili flakes

½ tsp (2 mL) smoked paprika

½ cup (125 mL) dry white wine

1½ lb (700 g) Russet potatoes, peeled and cut into ½-inch (1 cm) cubes

Salt to taste

Pepper to taste

6–8 cups (1.5–2 L) chicken or vegetable stock, divided

1 bunch kale (Tuscan or curly), ribs removed and very thinly sliced

1–2 Tbsp (30 mL) apple cider vinegar, lemon juice or white wine

½ cup (125 mL) chopped fresh parsley, for garnish

1. Preheat a stockpot over medium heat, add 2 Tbsp (30 mL) olive oil and sauté chorizo until crispy and browned, about 5–7 minutes. Remove with a slotted spoon and set aside.
2. Keeping the same pot over medium heat, add chopped onions to the chorizo-flavoured oil and sauté until softened, stirring occasionally, about 3 minutes. Add additional oil if needed.
3. Stir in garlic, chili flakes and smoked paprika; sauté for 1 minute.
4. Pour in white wine and reduce, making the onions look nice and saucy, about 1 minute. Add potatoes and stir to coat. Sauté potatoes for another 3 minutes until they just start to soften, then season with a good pinch of salt and pepper.
5. Pour in 6 cups (1.5 L) stock, bring to a boil, lower to simmer and cook until the potatoes start to fall apart when pricked with a fork, about 20 minutes.
6. Turn off heat and purée with a hand-immersion blender. I like to hold the pot with a tea towel in one hand, tilting so the blender is deeper into the soup to prevent splattering. Alternately, you can transfer to a food processor or blender for a smoother consistency.
7. Once puréed, place the pot back on heat and adjust consistency with the additional 2 cups (500 mL) stock. For a thicker, heartier soup, leave as is. I like it thinner, so I end up using the additional stock. Taste and check seasoning. Add more salt, pepper or chili flakes, if desired.
8. Add thinly sliced kale and simmer until greens are tender, about 5 minutes.
9. Pour in a splash of apple cider vinegar, lemon juice or white wine to boost the flavour.
10. Add the chorizo back into the soup just before serving and garnish each bowl with chopped parsley.

CALDO VERDE TIP

- You can use thinly sliced cabbage or collards instead of kale.

(GF, NF, LS)

POT OF CHILI

Chili is what I crave when the weather starts to get cold. A hearty chili packed with flavour is sure to warm up your belly. This one has bacon and smoked paprika, but it is also packed with vegetables and, depending on how much heat you like, I have added the optional ingredient of a chipotle pepper.

Chili is always better the next day and freezes so well, so think about making it on a weekend for a quick weeknight dinner. It is also great packed in a Thermos with tortilla chips on the side for dipping.

MAKES 6 servings
PREP TIME 10 minutes
COOK TIME 40 minutes

- 7½ oz (220 g) bacon, diced
- 17 oz (500 g) ground beef
- 1 large onion, finely diced
- 2 cloves garlic, chopped
- 1 cup (250 mL) diced carrots (about 2–3)
- 2 celery, diced
- 2 bay leaves
- 1 Tbsp (15 mL) ground cumin
- 1 Tbsp (15 mL) chili powder
- 1 Tbsp (15 mL) dried oregano
- 1 tsp (5 mL) smoked paprika
- 1 tsp (5 mL) ground cinnamon
- 2¼ oz (70 g) tomato paste (half of a 5½-oz/165-g can)
- ½–1 chipotle pepper in adobo, finely diced (optional)
- 15-oz (425 g) can black beans, rinsed and drained
- 3 cups (750 mL) chicken or beef stock
- 1 red or green pepper, diced
- Salt to taste
- Pepper to taste
- Sour cream or plain yogurt, for garnish
- 2–3 Tbsp (45 mL) chopped coriander, for garnish
- 1 lime cut in wedges, for garnish
- 2–3 thinly sliced green onions, for garnish

1. In a Dutch oven or large saucepot with a lid, fry bacon over medium heat until crispy, about 6–8 minutes. With a slotted spoon transfer to a paper towel–lined plate.
2. In the same pot over medium-high heat, brown beef in bacon fat. Transfer to another paper towel–lined plate with a slotted spoon.
3. Sauté onions in the same bacon fat over medium heat until translucent, about 3 minutes. Stir in the garlic, carrots and celery. Sauté for another 3–5 minutes, until slightly softened.
4. Stir in spices and toast for 1 minute. Stir in tomato paste and cook for 2–3 minutes. Add chipotle, if using.
5. Add beans, return beef to the pot and pour over enough stock to just cover the chili. Reduce heat to low and simmer.
6. Add in chopped pepper, season with salt and pepper and simmer, covered, for 15–20 minutes or until vegetables are tender.
7. Stir in bacon and garnishes, taste and adjust seasoning if necessary.

CHILI TIPS

- Try making this chili with any ground meat you like. Substitute extra-firm tofu for meat or double the amount of vegetables for a vegetarian alternative.
- Use any can of beans you like. I love the texture of the little black beans and they retain their shape better than kidney beans.
- Don't forget the toppings. Bring out all the suggested garnishes, so folks can load them on.

COOL FACT: CHIPOTLES IN ADOBO PACK A LOT OF HEAT BUT ALSO HAVE A TON OF FLAVOUR

These little tins, found in the Mexican section of your grocery store, are smoked dried jalapenos stored in an amazing intense spicy tomato sauce. Start out with half of one pepper in a stew then adjust, adding more as you like. You will never use a whole tin in a recipe, but they will keep stored in the fridge for a few weeks, or you can store in smaller portions in the freezer.

(V, NF, LS)

LEMON DROP SOUP WITH TEENY PASTA (PASTINA)

If you have kids, you probably have a mother-in-law, or in my case, an ex-mother-in-law. In my early days of becoming a wife, mother and cook, she was a huge help. She also was the one who stressed the importance of family dinners, which were always impressive and hard to live up to. I remember the day I had her version of this simple classic Jewish lemon egg soup, also known as Greek Avgolemono. It is a comforting no-cream creamy soup with a hint of lemon that is especially soothing during cold and flu season.

Well, here's my version. Served as more of a broth than a stew, I cook the pasta or long-grain rice separately, then add to the bowl when served. This way, if you have leftovers, the pasta doesn't swell and get mushy. I do this with almost every soup I make that has rice or pasta involved.

MAKES 4 servings
PREP TIME 10 minutes
COOK TIME 15 minutes

½ cup (125 mL) pastina (teeny pasta shapes like stars, balls, orzo, farfallini or letters of the alphabet) or long-grain rice

4 tsp (20 mL) olive oil, divided

½ onion, finely diced

2 cloves garlic, minced

2 medium carrots, small dice

2 celery stalks, small dice

5 sprigs of fresh thyme

Salt to taste

Pepper to taste

4 cups (1 L) chicken stock

2 eggs

2 Tbsp (30 mL) fresh lemon juice

1. In a small saucepot, cook pastina in boiling salted water according to the package instructions. Strain, put back into the pot and stir in 1 tsp (5 mL) olive oil to prevent sticking.
2. In a large saucepot over medium heat, sauté onion in the remaining olive oil until just softened, about 3 minutes. Stir in garlic and sauté for another 2 minutes, making sure not to brown.
3. Add carrots, celery and fresh thyme sprigs; season lightly with salt and pepper and sauté to soften slightly, about 3–5 minutes.
4. Pour in chicken stock and simmer until the vegetables are tender crisp, about 7–10 minutes. Remove from heat.
5. Whisk eggs with lemon juice in a medium-sized bowl. Slowly pour in 1 cup (250 mL) hot stock from the soup while whisking the eggs, then slowly pour mixture back into the soup while stirring. This method, called tempering, ensures your eggs don't curdle.
6. Place soup back over low heat for a few minutes and stir to heat through. Remove thyme sprigs. Taste and adjust seasoning. Note: if reheating soup, be sure to heat on low and do not boil or the eggs will scramble.
7. Portion pastina or rice into serving bowls then ladle soup overtop.

LEMON DROP SOUP TIP

- Use long-grain rice or gluten-free pasta for a wheat-free version.

COOL FACT: WHAT IT MEANS TO TEMPER

In the cooking world this has two meanings: 1) the process of slowly adding hot liquid to eggs so as not to cook or curdle them, or 2) the process of heating and cooling chocolate to stabilize it for chocolate making.

EASY SIDES

Vegetables are, for me, the most important part of a meal. Many nights I try to make vegetables the star of the table. Sometimes, on weekends, lunch is our big meal of the day, leaving dinner refreshingly simple and healthy—a simple side dish or soup can easily be dinner.

Prepping vegetables will take up the bulk of your time on a busy weeknight guaranteed, so here is the number one tip that has saved my life when I know I have a busy week coming up: as soon as I get home from the grocery store, I take half an hour to organize—trim stalks, wash lettuce, even peel and cut fruit and vegetables. Then I properly store everything, making meals easier to prepare throughout the week.

(GF, NF)

GLAZED CARROTS WITH POPPED MUSTARD SEEDS

Mustard seeds are one of my favourite secret ingredients. They have so much more to offer than the yellow squeeze bottles that sit in the fridge waiting for hot dogs. They add a subtle but fiery warmth, a little nuttiness and a tiny crunch. Mustard seeds are a key ingredient in curries and pickles, but they also really take a side of carrots to the next level. This is the simplest side for dinner parties, Thanksgiving or Christmas.

Gone are the days of boiled carrots with butter. Sweet, spicy and buttery—this is how carrots were meant to be enjoyed. Serve them on their own, over quinoa, with mashed potatoes or add the leftovers to your lunch salad the next day.

MAKES 4 servings
PREP TIME 5 minutes
COOK TIME 5 minutes

⅔ lb (350 g) carrots (about 5)

1 Tbsp (15 mL) olive oil

2 Tbsp (30 mL) yellow or brown mustard seeds

Salt to taste

Pepper to taste

1 Tbsp (15 mL) maple syrup or honey

⅓ cup (80 mL) water

1 Tbsp (15 mL) butter

1. Peel carrots and cut into coins or batons (sticks) that are 2 inches (5 cm) long by ½ inch (1 cm) wide.
2. Preheat a medium saucepot over medium heat, add olive oil, then mustard seeds. Cover with a lid and wait until you hear mustard seeds popping, 30 seconds to 1 minute.
3. Once popping, add carrots and stir to coat. Season lightly with salt and pepper; stir in maple syrup (or honey) and water. Cover and let simmer 5 minutes, or until tender crisp, adding a splash more water if necessary. You want the carrots to look glazed but not stick to the bottom of pot.
4. Finish with the butter over medium heat, tossing gently, until carrots are glistening. Taste and season with more salt and pepper if needed.

MUSTARD SEED TIP

- The trick with mustard seeds is you have to toast them in oil first. This helps release their fiery flavour. Once they start popping around in the pan, they're good to go, just don't leave them any longer or they will overcook and turn bitter.

COOL FACT: BUY CARROTS WITH THEIR TOPS ON

This is how you know they are really fresh. However, if you buy carrots with the tops on, trim tops before storing in a plastic bag in the fridge. The tops drink up the nutrients and water from the carrots, making them rubbery quickly.

(GF, NF, LS)

FIVE-MINUTE SAUTÉED GREEN BEANS

My daughter convinced me to include this recipe in the cookbook. Every time I make them, either for friends or family, someone always asks, "What did you do to those green beans?" I usually say nothing. Well, here is what I usually do to my green beans.

MAKES 4 side servings
PREP TIME 5 minutes, depending on whether or not you want to trim them (honestly, sometimes I don't)
COOK TIME 5 minutes

- 13 oz (400 g) green beans, trimmed
- 1 Tbsp (15 mL) olive oil
- Salt to taste
- Pepper to taste
- 1 Tbsp (15 mL) butter
- 2 Tbsp (30 mL) hemp hearts or sesame seeds (optional)

1. Plunge green beans into a large pot of boiling salted water and cook for 2 minutes. Drain well in a colander.
2. While beans are simmering, preheat a large sauté pan over high heat. Once super hot, add oil, then drained green beans. Season with salt and pepper and continue to sauté for about 3 minutes over high heat until seared.
3. Remove from heat, add butter to the pan and swirl so it melts and coats the beans. Plate and serve with a sprinkle of hemp or sesame seeds.

SAVED MY LIFE: BLANCHING AND SHOCKING VEGETABLES

Blanching and shocking vegetables is the easiest way to clean them while preserving flavour, colour, crunch and tenderness. To blanch means to plunge food for a brief period of time in boiling salted water. To shock means to stop the cooking process by running under cold water or plunging in an ice bath.

If I have a busy week coming up, right after my grocery shop I will take some extra time to prep vegetables like green beans, broccoli or carrots, then blanch them in batches. I store them in airtight containers in the fridge for quick preparations throughout the week. This way it is easier to throw them in a salad, pasta or grain dish.

GREEN BEAN TIP

- Green beans can be quickly trimmed of their tiny stems with kitchen shears or scissors and the help of a willing (or bribed) child.

(V, GF, NF, LS)

SICHUAN FIVE-SPICE KABOCHA WEDGES

So, what is kabocha? Well, you may never eat butternut squash again. This typically dark-green, tough-skinned, flat and gnarly-looking squash (also known as Japanese pumpkin) is awesome. Intensely sweet with a dark orange flesh so dense it almost seems dry, it reminds me of a cross between a sweet potato and a chestnut. I never peel it; when cooked, its skin softens and is completely edible, full of fibre and very nutritious. Squashes and pumpkin alike are known to be a source of beta-carotene, have anti-inflammatory properties and help regulate blood sugar, so I am always looking for new ways to work them into my meals. Try these wedges alongside my Orange Sumac Yogurt Dip (see p. 27), or cut leftovers into chunks and toss into a salad the next day.

MAKES 4 servings
PREP TIME 5 minutes
COOK TIME 20 minutes
SPECIAL EQUIPMENT NEEDED sharp chef's knife

2–3 lb (0.9–1.4 kg) green or red kabocha squash, washed, peel on

2 Tbsp (30 mL) olive oil or melted coconut oil

2 tsp (10 mL) Chinese five spice

1 tsp (5 mL) ground Sichuan pepper

½ tsp (2 mL) chili power

Salt to taste

1. Preheat oven to 425°F (220°C) and line or grease a baking sheet.
2. Using a chef's knife, slice off a thin section of the stem or root end of the squash, providing a flat surface to help cut the squash in half. Cut in half and scrape out the seeds with a spoon. Cut into quarters and, using the flat surface on a cutting board, cut into 1-inch (2.5 cm) wedges.
3. In a large bowl, stir together the remaining ingredients. Toss wedges in a bowl with the spiced oil to coat. Place in a single layer on the lined baking sheet and roast for 20 minutes, turning halfway through cooking time, until golden and fork tender.

SAVED MY LIFE: ONE GOOD SHARP KNIFE

It is true what they say, a dull knife is more dangerous than a sharp one. A blunt knife slips easily off food and you use your strength instead of the knife's sharpness to cut. This is a hazard, not to mention it slows you down. Everyone should have one good, preferably 8-inch (20 cm) chef's knife, and sharpen it regularly. Then go buy yourself a bread knife and a paring knife. Don't be afraid to let your kids get used to using knives. Start them off with a simple paring knife and teach them to keep their fingers tucked in like a claw.

KABOCHA TIPS

- Kabocha grows with both dark green and red skin. The red (more dark orange) tends to be a little sweeter.
- Sometimes mislabelled as buttercup squash or vice versa, kabocha have flat bottoms, whereas buttercup have a buttercup flower shape on the bottom.
- Squash will store up to 3 months in a cool dark place and up to 1 month at room temperature. There is no excuse not to have a few kicking around your house.
- Use kabocha the same as you would any other squash or pumpkin—steamed, puréed or made into a curry or even a pie.

(GF, NF, LS)

GARLIC CAULIFLOWER MASH

Cauliflower is always on the grocery list since it is in heavy rotation in our house. It's cheap, can feed a crowd and is extremely versatile. Both my sister and my kids demanded a recipe for cauliflower mash in this cookbook. Everyone loves it.

MAKES 4 servings
PREP TIME 5 minutes
COOK TIME 8–10 minutes
SPECIAL EQUIPMENT NEEDED steamer

1 lb (450 g) cauliflower (1 small head or ½ large head)

¼ cup (60 mL) butter

2 cloves garlic, finely chopped

¼ tsp (1 mL) freshly ground nutmeg

Salt to taste

Pepper to taste

1. Place a steamer insert or basket over boiling salted water. Quarter cauliflower and remove the core; break into large florets and steam, covered, until fork tender, about 8 minutes.
2. While cauliflower is steaming, melt butter in a small saucepot over medium-low heat until foamy. Add garlic and cook until softened and fragrant, about 5 minutes. Do not let it burn.
3. Once cauliflower is tender, transfer to a serving bowl and add warm garlic butter, nutmeg, salt and pepper. Mash to desired consistency.

CAULIFLOWER TIPS

- Nothing's wrong with cauliflower if it has a few brown spots on it. Trim them off if they bother you.
- The texture for a mash is a debatable topic. Some like more of a purée while others, like me, prefer it chunky.

COOL FACT: SALTING THE WATER HELPS EVEN WHEN STEAMING

Steaming vegetables over salted water may seem unnecessary but it does actually make a difference. Many chefs not only add salt but herbs, booze and other aromatics to the water while steaming. It adds flavour.

(V, GF, NF, LS)

ROAST SWEET POTATO COINS WITH THYME

As much as I love sweet potato fries, cutting them into coins with their skins left on means I can get them into the oven faster. We have always eaten sweet potatoes with the skins on, so it is just the norm in my house. They get beautifully golden brown on both sides and the aromatic thyme is not overwhelming and perfectly balances out the sweetness of the potatoes.

MAKES 4–6 servings
PREP TIME 6–8 minutes
COOK TIME 20 minutes

4 medium sweet potatoes, scrubbed, skin on and cut into ¼-inch (6 mm) wide coins (circles)

3 Tbsp (45 mL) fresh thyme leaves (about 15 sprigs)

2–3 Tbsp (45 mL) melted coconut oil or olive oil

Salt to taste

Pepper to taste

1 tsp (5 mL) Espelette (see Espelette Pepper Tip p. 141) or chili powder

1. Preheat oven to 425°F (220°C). Grease or line a baking sheet.
2. Place sweet potato coins in a large bowl and toss with the thyme, oil, salt, pepper and chili to coat.
3. Transfer to the baking sheet and place coins in an even layer. Roast until tender and golden brown on both sides, tossing halfway through roasting time—takes about 20 minutes.

(V, GF, NF)

COCONUT RICE

Rice is one of my favourite side dishes because it's quick, simple and can be served with almost anything. There are so many different kinds—long-grain, short-grain, wild, brown, etc.—that it's hard to pick just one. I like to switch it up and work as many of them into rotation as I can, but for this coconut sticky rice I am sticking to my guns and using jasmine. Its light floral aroma and soft clingy texture are the perfect match for rich coconut milk and fragrant spices.

MAKES 4 servings
SOAK TIME 30 minutes or overnight (optional)
COOK TIME 20 minutes
SPECIAL EQUIPMENT NEEDED saucepot with tight fitting lid or rice cooker

¾ cup (185 mL) coconut milk

¾ cup (185 mL) water

Pinch of salt

1 cup (250 mL) jasmine rice, rinsed and drained (preferably soaked for at least 30 minutes in water)

1 star anise

3 whole allspice

2 bay leaves

2 Tbsp (30 mL) sesame seeds, for garnish

2 Tbsp (30 mL) green onions, for garnish

1. In a medium saucepot bring all ingredients, except garnishes, to a boil; turn down to simmer and cover for 15–20 minutes, until liquid is absorbed and rice is tender.
2. Turn off heat and let stand, covered, for an additional 5 minutes.
3. Remove allspice and star anise. Fluff and serve with garnishes.

SAVED MY LIFE: PANTRY STAPLES

A well-stocked pantry with things like rice, canned beans, dried pasta and a few bottled sauces means there is always something I can pull together. Quite honestly, my kids couldn't be happier when there is a pot of plain rice on the stove and a few raw vegetables.

LONG-GRAIN RICE TIPS

- Soak rice in water if you have the time, but always rinse well. This removes excess starch or debris left on the rice from processing.
- Ratio of rice to water is 1 cup (250 mL) rice to 1½ cups (375 mL) water.
- After cooking, always let rice stand off heat, covered, for 5–30 minutes. While the rice is resting, it still continues to cook, soaking in and distributing moisture.
- A good pinch of salt and 2 Tbsp (30 mL) butter added during cooking makes all the difference to plain old rice.

(GF, NF, LS)

BRUSSELS SPROUTS, WHITE ASPARAGUS AND CRISPY BACON VINAIGRETTE

Having a hard time getting your family to eat Brussels sprouts or asparagus?

Drenching them with a crispy bacon vinaigrette is one way to win them over. The halving and quartering of the sprouts increases the surface caramelization, which means more browned bits of goodness. White asparagus is not as common as green, but don't pass it by in the veggie aisle. Give it a try. It is milder, more tender and has just as many nutrients as its green neighbour.

MAKES 4 sides
PREP TIME 10 minutes
COOK TIME 15 minutes
SPECIAL EQUIPMENT NEEDED large cast-iron or good sauté pan

½ lb (250 g) bacon, diced

1 lb (450 g) Brussels sprouts, trimmed, quartered if large or halved if small

1 bunch white or green asparagus, trimmed and cut into 1-inch (2.5 cm) pieces

Salt to taste

Pepper to taste

1 Tbsp (15 mL) Dijon mustard

2 Tbsp (30 mL) white wine vinegar

3 Tbsp (45 mL) extra virgin olive oil

1 Tbsp (15 mL) maple syrup (optional)

1. Put diced bacon in a large sauté or cast-iron pan and place over medium-low heat, stirring occasionally until crispy, about 6–8 minutes. Push bacon to one side and tilt the pan so that the fat drains and collects on the other side. Spoon out 2 Tbsp (30 mL) bacon fat and set aside in a bowl for the vinaigrette. Remove crispy bacon with a slotted spoon and set aside.
2. While cooking bacon, start boiling a large pot of salted water. Once boiling, add the Brussels sprouts and simmer for 3–4 minutes until tender crisp. Drain well.
3. Place the same dirty pan you cooked the bacon in, with any leftover bacon fat remaining, over high heat. When piping hot, add asparagus and Brussels sprouts. Season with salt and pepper and sear, about 5 minutes, stirring occasionally. Add a drizzle of olive oil if pan starts to look dry.
4. Make bacon vinaigrette with the reserved 2 Tbsp (30 mL) bacon fat, Dijon, vinegar, olive oil and maple syrup. Whisk until emulsified.
5. Transfer the sautéed sprouts and asparagus to a serving bowl and, while warm, pour the vinaigrette overtop and toss in the reserved crispy bacon. Serve.

SAVED MY LIFE: BACON
If you put bacon on anything your kids will at least try it.

BACON TIP

- Bacon doesn't like preheated pans. Toss (preferably at room temperature) bacon into a pan and put it over medium-low to medium heat. You want the bacon to render slowly. This way you will have rendered most of the fat before it gets all crispy.

ASPARAGUS TIPS

- Thin asparagus spears are better than thick ones. They are more tender and cook quicker.
- The tough woody ends will naturally snap off when bent with fingers near the bottom of the stems.
- In fancy restaurants they peel asparagus. Yes, it's cool, but I have never done this at home.
- Store longer by snapping off the tough woody stems and storing upright in a bowl or jar with 1 inch (2.5 cm) of water in the fridge.

(V, GF, NF, LS)

POLE AND BUSH BEAN SALAD WITH CRISPY CHICKPEAS

This salad is NOT your mom's "three-bean salad"—it is so much more! With tender pole beans, crispy chickpeas and a tangy maple syrup vinaigrette, this elevated classic is sure to become a new family favourite. I chalk it up to the crispy chickpeas. My kids absolutely love them in the salad or by the handful, and after you make this recipe once you'll understand why.

Served at room temperature or cold, this colourful bowl of beany goodness is the ideal summer salad for barbecues, picnics and potlucks.

MAKES 4 servings as a main or 6 as a side
PREP TIME 5 minutes
COOK TIME 10 minutes
SPECIAL EQUIPMENT NEEDED slotted spoon or spider spoon (see Saved My Life p. 13)

1 lb (450 g) pole runner beans, ends trimmed and beans cut into 2-inch (5 cm) pieces

1 lb (450 g) green, yellow or burgundy beans, trimmed

1 red or yellow pepper, diced

15 oz (450 g) can chickpeas, drained and rinsed

1–2 Tbsp (30 mL) olive oil

½ tsp (2 mL) smoked paprika

½ tsp (2 mL) chili powder

Salt to taste

Pepper to taste

⅓ cup (80 mL) slivered raw almonds or raw pumpkin seeds, for garnish

MAPLE VINAIGRETTE

1 tsp (5 mL) maple syrup or honey

2 Tbsp (30 mL) white wine vinegar

2 Tbsp (30 mL) extra virgin olive oil

½ clove garlic, puréed

½ shallot, finely diced

Salt to taste

1. In a large pot of boiling salted water, simmer all beans for 2–3 minutes, or until tender crisp. Transfer beans with a slotted spoon or spider spoon into a bowl of ice-cold water to stop cooking process.
2. Drain all beans, place on a clean tea towel and towel dry, absorbing excess moisture. Place beans into a serving bowl along with the diced pepper.
3. In a separate bowl, toss the chickpeas with 1 Tbsp (15 mL) olive oil and the smoked paprika, chili powder, salt and pepper to coat.
4. Place a large sauté pan over high heat. Once preheated, add the chickpeas and sauté for about 5 minutes until golden and crispy, adding more olive oil if necessary. Transfer to a paper towel–lined bowl and set aside.
5. To make the vinaigrette, place all ingredients into a small glass jar with a lid. Shake vigorously. Taste and adjust seasonings.
6. Toss the green beans with the vinaigrette. Sprinkle over the crispy chickpeas and garnish with a handful of nuts and/or seeds. Serve at room temperature or cold.

SAVED MY LIFE: MAKING VINAIGRETTES IN MASON JARS

Just put all ingredients in a jar, shake, use what you need then store leftovers in the fridge.

GREEN BEAN TIPS

- What's the difference between pole and bush beans? Pole beans, like the flatter longer pole runner beans, grow up and up and up like the ones in "Jack and the Beanstalk." Bush beans produce beans on bushes about 2 feet tall. This is where we get the most common green bean, also found in yellow and burgundy varieties.
- It's easier to trim green beans with scissors and to delegate this task to any bored meandering child.

(V, GF, NF, LS)

CRISPY SHALLOTS AND GARLIC CHIPS

There is not a lot of deep-frying happening in my house. I can never think of a good enough reason to deal with all that oil. However, I do make an exception for these crispy shallots and garlic chips. They are two of my all-time favourite garnishes.

It doesn't take a huge amount of oil to fry these thin slices of shallots and garlic. Also, the oil that you do use can be reused. You will end up with a flavoured oil to drizzle overtop meat, steamed veggies and salads, or to use as a dip for bread.

It is the same method for both recipes. If you decide you want to make both you can use the same oil—just fry in batches since the shallots and garlic will have slightly different fry times.

MAKES about ¾ cup (185 mL)
PREP TIME 5 minutes
COOK TIME 5 minutes
SPECIAL EQUIPMENT NEEDED slotted spoon or spider spoon, fine mesh sieve, digital thermometer (optional)

1½ cups (375 mL) neutral-flavoured oil (approx.)

5 shallots (about ½ lb/250 g), halved, thinly sliced and pulled apart into rings or 8–12 garlic cloves, thinly sliced

Salt to taste

1. In a medium saucepot, add 1 inch (2.5 cm) oil. Heat over medium high until the oil registers 350°F (175°C). No thermometer? Test oil with a slice of shallot or garlic. If it sizzles, it's ready. Don't let the oil get to the point where it's smoking.
2. Fry shallots or garlic until lightly golden. Use a fork to stir occasionally for even frying; they will continue to cook and crisp up as they cool. Strain over a heat-proof bowl, reserving flavoured oil for another use.
3. Transfer to a paper towel-lined plate and season with salt.
4. Store in an airtight container for up to a month. Mine doesn't last past dinner.

FRYING TIPS

- Fry in pots with high sides. The oil can bubble up and overflow in shallow pans.
- Use oils with a high smoke point like grapeseed, avocado or rice bran oil. Smoking oil creates a burnt flavour and releases harmful free radicals.
- The ideal frying temperature is 340–375°F (165–190°C).
- Batch fry and avoid overcrowding the pot. The more you add to the pot, the more it brings down the oil's temperature.
- Once oil smokes it means it's burnt and needs to be discarded (not down the sink). Dispose of oil according to city rules and regulations. Cooled and put in an old plastic container with a lid and thrown in the garbage works.

COOL FACT: RICE BRAN OIL IS GOOD FOR HIGH TEMPERATURE COOKING

Otherwise known as rice bran extract, rice bran oil has a smoke point of 490°F (255°C) and a very neutral taste. I have only been able to find it in health food stores but it is relatively inexpensive. You can easily purchase it online.

(V, GF, NF, LS)

ALL-DRESSED KALE CHIPS

What was life like before kale chips? Where did they come from? Who invented them? It seems that recipes for crispy kale can only be found dating back, at the most, 5 years. Now grocery stores sell them prepackaged for a small fortune, but you should just make your own. It's so easy. They take only minutes to bake and a large bunch of kale will only set you back a couple bucks. They are addictive, take on almost any flavour and are a healthy snack option.

I use them as a topping or garnish as well as a snack, and kids seem to love them. Thank God.

Once again, you will see me using ground sumac here. It adds a zesty citrus zing without getting the kale leaves all wet with lemon juice.

MAKES about 6 cups (1.5 L)
PREP TIME 10 minutes
COOK TIME 15–20 minutes
SPECIAL EQUIPMENT very large bowl

- 1 large bunch curly kale, stems removed and leaves torn into chip-sized pieces
- 2 Tbsp (30 mL) melted coconut oil or extra virgin olive oil
- 2 Tbsp (30 mL) nutritional yeast or grated Parmesan cheese (or to taste)
- 1 tsp (5 mL) garlic powder
- ½ tsp (2 mL) onion powder
- 1 tsp (5 mL) smoked paprika
- ½ tsp (2 mL) chili powder
- 2 tsp (10 mL) ground sumac
- Pepper to taste

1. Preheat oven to 300°F (150°C). Line a baking sheet.
2. In a very large bowl, using hands, massage oil into all the nooks and crannies of the kale leaves. You want the kale to be evenly coated but not slathered in oil.
3. Sprinkle remaining ingredients on the kale and massage again. Taste and adjust seasoning if you wish.
4. Spread kale in a single, even layer on a baking sheet; use 2 baking sheets if you have them, or do in batches.
5. Bake 5 minutes, rotate pan(s) and swap racks if using 2 baking sheets, then bake for another 5 minutes. Keep an eye on the chips for the last few minutes. Once edges are slightly brown, remove. Kale chips may not look entirely crispy at this point but will crisp further as they cool.

KALE CHIP TIPS

- Don't throw away your stems. Keep stems to throw in smoothies or soups, or finely chop to sauté or stir fry with other vegetables.
- Make sure kale is washed and dried. Salad spinners are great for this. Any dressing or oil will stick better to dry leaves than wet.
- Got a dehydrator? Use it. Kale chips take approximately 4 hours at 115°F (45°C).

MAINS

I was going to separate this into sections like Meat, Chicken, Fish, etc., but I decided to keep it simple and include all these under one heading: Mains. Like in a restaurant, this chapter covers what one would consider the main course in a meal. Recipes cover different cooking techniques and range from simple to spectacular.

I wanted this chapter to cover a bit of everything, all of which can be served as a main. However, as you will see after perusing this chapter, some of these dishes crossover into sides or nice one-dish wonders that can be eaten for lunch or dinner. All of these recipes I have served and shared at one point or another with my family and friends.

(NF, LS)

CAULIFLOWER MAC AND CHEESE WITH PROSCIUTTO

This is my lightened up version of a comfort food classic—and an obvious favourite around the dinner table at my house. Think mac and cheese meets cauliflower with cheese sauce. The best part is that there is a whole head of cauliflower in this recipe, so you're getting a good serving of vegetables with every bite.

MAKES 6–8 servings
PREP TIME 40 minutes
COOK TIME 20 minutes
SPECIAL EQUIPMENT NEEDED casserole dish (9 × 9 inches/23 × 23 cm) or a large cast-iron pan, blender or food processor

¼ lb (125 g) sliced prosciutto, roughly chopped

2 cups (500 mL) brown rice macaroni

1 large head of cauliflower, cut into large florets

1 cup (250 mL) chicken stock

3 Tbsp (45 mL) butter + extra for greasing the casserole dish

½ onion, grated

2 cloves garlic, puréed

3 Tbsp (45 mL) all-purpose flour

1½ cups (375 mL) whole milk

1 Tbsp (15 mL) Dijon mustard

½ tsp (2 mL) cayenne

1 tsp (5 mL) smoked paprika

Freshly grated nutmeg to taste

1 cup (250 mL) grated medium cheddar cheese

1 cup (250 mL) grated Gruyère cheese

Salt to taste

Pepper to taste

¾ cup (185 mL) grape tomatoes, cut in half

⅓ cup (80 mL) grated Parmesan (approx.), for topping

All-Dressed Kale Chips (see p. 99), for garnish (optional)

1. Preheat oven to 400°F (200°C) and grease a casserole dish or cast-iron frying pan with butter.
2. Preheat the sauté pan over medium-high heat. Add chopped prosciutto and cook until crispy, about 2–3 minutes. Set aside in a bowl.
3. Boil pasta in boiling salted water, according to the package directions; drain and set aside.
4. Steam cauliflower florets over boiling salted water in a double boiler (or steamer insert) until fork tender. Transfer half of the steamed cauliflower into a blender or food processor and purée with the stock until smooth. Chop remaining cauliflower florets into smaller florets.
5. In a large saucepot, melt butter over medium-low heat until foamy. Add onion and garlic, and cook 3–5 minutes until softened.
6. Stir in flour and continue to cook, while stirring, for 3 minutes.
7. Slowly whisk in milk to prevent lumps from forming, whisk in cauliflower purée and continue to simmer over medium heat, stirring occasionally until thickened, about 3–5 minutes.
8. Whisk in the Dijon, cayenne, paprika and nutmeg. Add the grated cheddar and Gruyère cheese and keep on low heat until melted. Season with salt and pepper.
9. Fold the cooked pasta, chopped cauliflower and prosciutto into the cheese sauce. Spoon into a greased dish.
10. Sprinkle Parmesan overtop and scatter with halved grape tomatoes. Bake approximately 20 minutes or until bubbling and browned on top.

11. Serve with All-Dressed Kale Chips (see p. 99) sprinkled on top, if desired.

CAULIFLOWER MAC AND CHEESE TIPS

- For next-level cauliflower mac and cheese, roast the cauliflower instead of steaming it; this will bring out the natural sugars, giving it a rich caramelized flavour. Toss the florets lightly with olive oil, salt and pepper to taste, then roast on a sheet pan at 425°F (220°C) until tender and golden, approx. 20 minutes. This is a great recipe if you have any leftover roasted or streamed cauliflower.
- You can always add more cheese.

COOL FACT: WHAT IS A ROUX

The pasty concoction of butter (or any fat) and flour used in this recipe is called a "roux" and it is used as a base to thicken many cream sauces—think Béchamel. Typically equal parts fat and flour are mixed, then cooked to rid the mixture of any raw flour flavour until a desired colour, like blonde or brown, is reached.

(GF, NF, LS)

MOROCCAN CHICKEN THIGHS

Chicken is the most popular choice of meat, which can get a little boring, but the exotic aroma and intense flavour of this super-simple-yet-vibrant Moroccan spice blend takes those boring, inexpensive chicken thighs to a whole other level. Everyone who has tried these asks me for the recipe. Marinate the night before or in the morning before heading off to work. This is an easy choice for any weeknight meal.

MAKES 4 servings
PREP TIME 5 minutes
MARINATE TIME 2 hours (minimum)
COOK TIME 15 minutes
SPECIAL EQUIPMENT NEEDED ovenproof skillet or fry pan with a roasting dish

- ½ lemon, juiced
- 1 Tbsp (15 mL) olive oil
- 1 tsp (5 mL) ground cumin
- 1 tsp (5 mL) ground coriander
- ½ tsp (2 mL) ground cinnamon
- ½ tsp (2 mL) ground turmeric
- ½ tsp (2 mL) chili powder
- ½ tsp (2 mL) smoked paprika
- 6 bone-in skin-on chicken thighs (about 2 lb/900 g)
- Salt to taste
- Pepper to taste
- 1 Tbsp (15 mL) neutral-flavoured oil
- Lemon wedges, for garnish
- 2 Tbsp (30 mL) chopped parsley, for garnish

1. In a large bowl, whisk together the lemon juice, olive oil, cumin, coriander, cinnamon, turmeric, chili powder and smoked paprika. Add the chicken thighs and toss to coat. Cover the bowl or place in a resealable plastic bag and marinate in the fridge for 2–3 hours.
2. Preheat oven to 375°F (190°C).
3. Remove chicken from the marinade and season both sides with salt and pepper. Preheat a large ovenproof skillet over high heat, add neutral-flavoured oil and sear thighs skin side down until skin is browned and crispy. Turn thighs over and transfer skillet to the oven for 10–15 minutes, until the internal temperature is 160°F (71°C) or juices run clear.
4. Rest 5 minutes before serving with lemon wedges and chopped parsley.

CHICKEN TIPS

- It's time to stop buying those crazy expensive boneless skinless chicken breasts. To me, chicken thighs are, by far, the better choice. Cheaper and juicier, they cook quickly and have more flavour.
- Cooking chicken with its skin on and bones in is not only cheaper, but the skin helps retain moisture and the bones give the chicken more flavour. Plus, the crispy skin is the best part.

COOL FACT: SALTING A MARINADE

Do you salt a marinade? The short answer here, for me, is that I am sensitive to salt, so I like to have as much control of it as possible. Therefore, no. I salt marinating meat just before cooking and then adjust towards the end of the cooking process if necessary. Chicken thighs are small to begin with, and this marinade is so flavourful that salt isn't needed to help penetrate the spices into the meat.

(GF, NF, LS)

HANDS-DOWN GO-TO MARINATED BEEF

This is the only beef marinade you need. Perfect for those tough cuts that need a little loosening up, your steak will love this robust flavour combination. The tamarind, soy and molasses give it that Worcestershire feel, but it's the unforgettable rosemary that will keep you coming back.

Thinly slice this beef with all its juices over a bed of peppery arugula and you have an instant winner. Any leftovers make an amazing steak sandwich.

MAKES enough for 1½ lb (700 g) beef
PREP TIME 5 minutes
COOK TIME 10 minutes
MARINATE TIME 4–24 hours

- 3 Tbsp (45 mL) olive oil
- 1 tsp (5 mL) soy
- 1 tsp (5 mL) molasses
- 1 Tbsp (15 mL) tamarind paste
- 1 Tbsp (15 mL) apple cider vinegar
- ⅛ tsp (0.5 mL) ground cloves
- ½ tsp (2 mL) dried chili flakes
- 2 cloves garlic, puréed
- 2 Tbsp (30 mL) grated onion (about ½ small or ¼ large onion)
- 2 Tbsp (30 mL) finely chopped rosemary
- Pepper to taste
- ½ tsp (2 mL) salt
- 1½ lb (700 g) flank, flat iron, skirt, hanger or bavette steak

1. Mix all ingredients together in a small bowl, making sure to break up the tamarind paste. Place marinade in a resealable plastic bag, add meat and create as much of an airtight seal as possible. Through the bag, massage marinade all over beef.
2. Marinate for at least 2 hours or up to 1 day in the fridge. If you can, let beef come to room temperature at least 1 hour before cooking. Season both sides lightly with salt.
3. Get the grill, a grill pan or a cast-iron pan very hot. Sear the beef on both sides, about 3 minutes per side, or until medium rare (135°F/57°C) or medium (145°F/63°C).
4. Remove from heat, let rest 5 minutes, slice against the grain and serve.

SAVED MY LIFE: BRAVING THE HEAT

One of the biggest obstacles to overcome in the kitchen was training myself to get used to working with heat. I was afraid to let a grill pan smoke or to leave a piece of meat searing without fiddling with it. Things cook faster and more evenly if the pan or oven is preheated properly, especially if you want a good sear. Also, think about this: how are you going to get a piece of meat beautifully caramelized if you keep moving the bloody thing around in the pan?

TAMARIND PASTE TIPS

- The fruit of the tamarind tree has been made into a sticky, sweet and sour, ready-to-use cooking paste that is used in everything from Thai to Mexican to Jamaican cooking. It is typically sold in blocks or tubs at most grocery stores in the spice section or Asian food aisle.
- Tamarind blocks can be stored at room temperature for up to 2 years. I store mine with all my spices.

(GF, NF, LS)

PORK MEDALLIONS WITH RED WINE JUNIPER SAUCE

If you like gin, you will love juniper. Its crisp, piney, peppery taste has a hint of citrus, and this bold red-wine juniper sauce smothered over simple juicy cumin-spiced pork is an impressive dish.

Pork tenderloin is amazingly versatile and super easy to cook, yet I find it often overlooked. This inexpensive prime cut is tender, lean, mildly flavoured, requires no marinating and can be cooked in 10 minutes. You could call it the "poor man's filet mignon," but that would discount its tremendous flavour.

Tenderloins vary in size and are sometimes sold two in a package. One 1½-lb (700 g) tenderloin is enough to feed a family of four but, by all means, double this recipe, because the leftovers are amazing.

MAKES 4 servings
PREP TIME 5 minutes
COOK TIME 15 minutes
SPECIAL EQUIPMENT NEEDED large ovenproof sauté pan, digital thermometer

1½ lb (700 g) pork tenderloin

Salt to taste

Pepper to taste

1–2 tsp (10 mL) ground cumin (or to taste)

1–2 Tbsp (30 mL) neutral-flavoured oil

5 sprigs fresh thyme

2 cloves garlic, smashed

3 Tbsp (45 mL) butter, divided

½ cup (125 mL) red wine

10 juniper berries, lightly crushed

1 cup (250 mL) beef or chicken stock

1. Preheat oven to 400°F (200°C).
2. Cut tenderloin into medallions (or small steaks) on the diagonal, about 1½ inches (4 cm) thick. You should get at least 4 medallions and 2 smaller end pieces. Season with salt, lots of pepper and ground cumin.
3. Heat an ovenproof pan over high heat. Once hot, add the oil and sear the medallions, about 3 minutes per side. Once turned over, add thyme sprigs, garlic and 1 Tbsp (15 mL) butter. Transfer to the oven for 6–10 minutes or until an internal temperature of 140°F (60°C) is reached. Smaller end pieces will cook more quickly, so remove ahead of time.
4. Remove pan from the oven, transfer pork onto a plate and let rest while making the pan sauce.
5. In the same pan over medium heat, add the wine, juniper berries and stock. Liquids will immediately start bubbling and reduce. Add in 2 Tbsp (30 mL) butter to finish the sauce. Taste and adjust seasoning if necessary with salt and pepper. Pour sauce over the medallions and serve.

PORK TIP

- Pork tenderloin, being so lean, is easily overcooked. This, again, is where I stress the value of a digital thermometer, which makes it so easy to cook meat properly. Take the pork out of the oven once it registers 140°F (60°C) in the middle of the thickest part and let it rest for 5 minutes. The result will be juicy pork with the slightest blush of pink.

COOL FACT: JUNIPER BERRIES AREN'T REALLY BERRIES

Juniper berries are used to make gin, so we know they must be good for us. The berry, which is actually a seed cone of the juniper tree, is typically sold whole in the spice section of your grocery store. They look like big dark purple peppercorns and are easily crushed, which should be done just before using. This helps to release the berry's essential oils.

(GF, NF, LS)

PARSNIP AND SWISS CHARD FRITTATA

If you have a carton of eggs and a few vegetables kicking around, you've got a meal. Frittatas are simple to make and can be served hot, at room temperature or cold, plus you can eat them for breakfast, lunch or dinner. Just follow the easy method below for a meal that can be served anytime, anywhere. Parsnips give a lighter feel than the traditionally used potatoes and, since my love affair with spinach has fizzled, I have recently been romanced by the slight peppery taste of Swiss chard.

Here is a great example of a recipe where a good ovenproof skillet, like a seasoned cast-iron pan, makes all the difference. Food is less likely to stick to the bottom and you get nice even cooking.

MAKES 6–8 servings
PREP TIME 20 minutes
COOK TIME 10–15 minutes
SPECIAL EQUIPMENT NEEDED large (preferably 10 inch/25 cm) ovenproof non-stick pan or seasoned cast-iron pan

- 1 bunch Swiss chard, stems removed (keep for another use), leafy greens only
- 2 Tbsp (30 mL) olive oil
- 1 onion, finely diced
- 1 clove garlic, finely chopped or puréed
- 2 large or 3 small parsnips, peeled and thinly sliced into coins
- 1 red pepper, finely diced
- 1 jalapeno, finely diced (optional)
- 8 eggs
- 1 cup (250 mL) heavy cream (35%)
- 1 Tbsp (15 mL) Dijon mustard
- 1 tsp (5 mL) salt
- Pepper to taste
- 2 Tbsp (30 mL) chopped fresh herbs such as chives, basil and/or parsley
- ¾ cup (185 mL) grated Swiss cheese or Gruyère

1. Preheat oven to 350°F (175°C).
2. In a large pot of boiling salted water, add Swiss chard and boil until just wilted, about 2 minutes. Drain and run under cold running water until cool enough to handle. Using your hands, squeeze out all excess water. Chop the chard and set aside.
3. Preheat an ovenproof non-stick or cast-iron pan over medium heat. Add the olive oil and sauté onion until softened, about 3 minutes. Stir in garlic and sauté for an additional 1 minute to soften. Add sliced parsnips and cook until just tender, stirring occasionally, about 5 minutes.
4. Add the chopped chard, red pepper and jalapeno, if using. Stir in the pan and create an even layer of mixed vegetables.
5. In a large bowl, whisk eggs with the cream, Dijon, salt, pepper and chopped herbs.
6. Lower heat to medium-low and pour the egg custard evenly over the vegetables. Cook, without stirring, until the edges start to set, about 5 minutes.
7. Sprinkle grated cheese overtop and transfer to the oven for 10–15 minutes, until centre is just set. The larger the pan, the thinner the frittata and the faster it will cook.
8. Cool 10 minutes before serving. Serve straight out of the pan or invert onto a serving platter. Enjoy hot, at room temperature or cold.

FRITTATA TIPS

- Leftover frittata sliced between two pieces of buttered toast is a pretty kick-ass breakfast to go.
- Certain vegetables release moisture when cooked, like spinach, chard and mushrooms. These will make frittatas watery if added in raw. Precook these types of ingredients and drain excess moisture before adding to your frittata.
- Dense ingredients, like parsnips and potatoes, should also be precooked to ensure they are tender after the frittata is baked.
- Don't have a kid old enough to run to the corner store for cream? Frittatas don't need cream or milk; however, the cream does create a more luscious consistency. No cream will just mean a denser frittata. If substituting milk or yogurt for cream, the fuller the fat the better.

(GF, NF, LS)

SUPER JUICY TURKEY SLIDERS

Having a hard time getting your kids to eat zucchini? Such a shame since it's cheap, available all year round and can be eaten raw, steamed, sautéed or grated and integrated (or hidden) into a recipe like these Super Juicy Turkey Sliders.

Here is a recipe I adapted that my kids love from Ottolenghi and Tamimi's Jerusalem cookbook. I just love its nutty, earthy, citrusy tones and how it pairs perfectly with cumin and fresh cilantro.

This is an ideal healthy protein-packed snack or main that can be eaten warm or cold. The lack of breadcrumbs makes it also ideal for any Paleo eaters out there. Try serving it with my simple Orange Sumac Yogurt Dip (see p. 27) or Homemade Hot Sauce (see p. 25).

MAKES 10–12 sliders
PREP TIME 10 minutes
COOK TIME 10 minutes
SPECIAL EQUIPMENT NEEDED portioner (disher) such as an ice cream scoop or measuring spoons, digital thermometer

- 1 egg, lightly beaten
- 1 clove garlic, puréed
- 1 tsp (5 mL) ground cumin
- 1 tsp (5 mL) ground coriander
- ¼ tsp (1 mL) cayenne
- 1 tsp (5 mL) salt
- Pepper to taste
- 3 green onions, finely chopped
- 1 cup (250 mL) coarsely grated zucchini
- 2 Tbsp (30 mL) chopped cilantro
- 1 lb (450 g) ground turkey or chicken
- 2–4 Tbsp (30–60 mL) neutral-flavoured oil
- Slider buns, pitas or lettuce cups (optional)

1. Preheat oven to 425°F (220°C) and line a baking sheet.
2. In a large bowl, lightly beat the egg with a fork. Stir in the garlic, spices, salt and pepper. Stir in green onions, zucchini and cilantro.
3. Add ground turkey and mix by hand until meat binds with all other ingredients. All this can be done ahead of time and cooked when needed, just cover with plastic wrap and transfer to the fridge.
4. Portion slider mix into equal-sized balls, about 2 Tbsp (30 mL) each, and place on another plate or baking sheet. Flatten each slightly to form mini patties.
5. Preheat a large cast-iron or sauté pan over medium-high heat. Add in 1 Tbsp (15 mL) oil and sear sliders on both sides, about 3 minutes per side. Do not over-crowd pan; this can be done in batches, adding more oil as needed. Transfer to a lined baking sheet and place in the oven for 5 minutes, or until the internal temperature reaches 165°F (74°C).
6. Serve warm or cold, with buns and condiments of choice.

SAVED MY LIFE: USING RECYCLED LIDS FROM JARS

No portioner? Use an appropriate-sized lid from a jar, lined with plastic wrap, to help form patties of equal size.

SLIDER AND BURGER TIPS

- Ground meat should always be kept cold until ready to cook. This way you will get a better sear and it prevents overcooking the meat inside.
- Use gentle hands; overpacking the meat when forming patties yields tough, dense burgers.

COOL FACT: YOU DON'T REALLY NEED TO BE BUYING THAT EXTRA-LEAN GROUND MEAT

Fat equals flavour. It has been drilled into our heads that leaner is better—buy lower fat this and that—but when it comes to making burgers, the fat is what is going to keep them juicy. Quality is better than quantity. Isn't it better to eat smaller portions of yummy food than large portions of food with no flavour?

(V, GF, NF)

SWEET AND SPICY SPAGHETTI SQUASH WITH SORGHUM

If you are craving pasta but trying to cut down on carbs then this roasted spaghetti squash served on top of a simple sorghum pilaf is just for you. Sorghum is full of iron and protein but my favourite thing about it is it reminds me of Israeli couscous or pasta balls when cooked. The lime, cilantro and avocado add a welcome freshness to the decadent roasted spaghetti squash.

MAKES 4 servings
PREP TIME 10 minutes
COOK TIME 1 hour

- 1 cup (250 mL) sorghum, rinsed
- 1 medium spaghetti squash (about 1 lb/450 g), cut in half, seeds removed
- 2 Tbsp (30 mL) honey or maple syrup
- 1 Tbsp (15 mL) sriracha or Homemade Hot Sauce (see p. 25)
- 2 Tbsp (30 mL) extra virgin olive oil + extra for the squash
- 1 Tbsp (15 mL) freshly squeezed lime juice
- Salt to taste
- Pepper to taste
- 1 Tbsp (15 mL) chopped cilantro or mint
- 1 Tbsp (15 mL) chopped chives
- 1 red pepper, finely diced
- 2 avocados, diced

1. Cook sorghum in boiling salted water the same as you would pasta for 1 hour or until tender.
2. Meanwhile, preheat oven to 425°F (220°C). Drizzle the inside of the spaghetti squash with olive oil and roast, flesh side down, on a lined baking sheet for about 20 minutes, until fork tender. Turn over, drizzle with honey or maple syrup and sriracha and place back in the hot oven to caramelize another 5 minutes. Let cool, scrape the spaghetti-like insides out with a fork into a bowl and set aside.
3. Once the sorghum is cooked, drain well and place in a serving bowl. Drizzle with olive oil and lime juice and season with salt and pepper to taste.
4. Toss in the chopped herbs, red pepper and avocado.
5. Serve with roasted spaghetti squash on top. Mix as you eat.

SORGHUM TIP

- I love cooking with this inexpensive superfood that is naturally high in iron, fibre, protein, magnesium and potassium. It is a great nutritious gluten-free pasta alternative.

(GF, NF)

MAPLE CANDY SALMON

This salmon is so indescribably good, you know there has to be a catch. It always turns out perfectly cooked, perfectly seasoned and tasting like candy. Leftovers are especially good served with scrambled eggs or over a simple salad of sprouts and greens. Your kids will love this salmon and it will leave everyone wanting more. I should have called it Maple Crack Salmon. It takes less than 5 minutes to prep and has only 3 ingredients, so, what's the catch? It takes 3 days to marinate. So plan ahead for your next big fish feast.

MAKES 4 servings
PREP TIME 5 minutes
MARINATE TIME 3 days
COOK TIME 6–8 minutes

4 tsp (20 mL) salt (you want 3 times as much salt as you would normally season with)

Four 6–8 oz (175–225 g) skinless boneless salmon or trout filets

¼ cup (60 mL) dark maple syrup

Pepper to taste

1. Salt filets liberally on all sides and place in an airtight container or resealable plastic bag. Add maple syrup; the salmon should be immersed in syrup. Cure salmon for 3 days in the fridge.
2. Preheat oven to 425°F (220°C) and line a baking sheet with foil. Take filets out of the syrup-salt mixture, add pepper to taste and place in the oven for 6–8 minutes, or until fish flakes easily and the outside is caramelized.

(GF, NF, LS)

GARLIC AND THYME ROAST CHICKEN BREASTS

I can't tell you how many times I have served these roast chicken breasts. They're easy enough for weeknight dinners but fancy enough that my friends insist I serve them at every dinner party. They come for my chicken.

There is something magical about garlicky, lots-of-thyme-butter-infused chicken. The simple trick to cooking perfectly juicy chicken is not overcooking it. This is where a digital thermometer really is your best friend.

Try serving this chicken with a simple salad, Glazed Carrots with Popped Mustard Seeds (see p. 88) and/or Garlic Cauliflower Mash (see p. 92).

MAKES 4 servings
PREP TIME 10 minutes
COOK TIME 20–25 minutes
SPECIAL EQUIPMENT NEEDED large ovenproof pan or a good sauté and roasting pan

- ¼ cup (60 mL) butter, softened
- 4 garlic cloves, puréed
- 16 sprigs fresh thyme, leaves only
- Salt to taste
- Pepper to taste
- 4 bone-in skin-on chicken breasts
- 1 Tbsp (15 mL) neutral-flavoured oil
- 1 large sweet onion (such as a Valencia), thinly sliced
- 1–1½ cups (375 mL) chicken stock

1. Preheat oven to 375°F (190°C).
2. Make a compound butter by stirring butter with the garlic, thyme, a good pinch of salt and pepper.
3. With fingers, create a pocket under the skin of each breast, starting at the thickest end. Divide the compound butter and push into each pocket. Season both sides of the chicken with salt and pepper.
4. Preheat a large ovenproof pan over high heat and add the oil sear; chicken breasts, skin side first, about 3 minutes until browned. Turn chicken over, scatter the sliced onion overtop and pour in 1 cup (250 mL) stock. If the pan cannot go in the oven, transfer seared chicken to a roasting pan, then add the onion and stock. Transfer to the oven for 20 minutes or until the internal temperature reaches 160°F (71°C). Check halfway through cooking time, adding a little more stock if the bottom of the pan looks dry.
5. Let chicken rest 5 minutes before serving; serve with sliced onions and pan juices overtop.

SAVED MY LIFE: LITTLE FINGERS ARE BETTER AT PICKING THYME LEAVES

I am not a big fan of chopping garlic and picking those tiny thyme leaves off their sprigs. This is why I use a microplane to purée garlic and get my kids to do the thyme. Little fingers are especially good for picking small thyme leaves, plus it provides an opportunity for kids to work on their dexterity. Win-win.

COMPOUND BUTTER TIPS

- This is simply butter that has flavours mixed into it, which can be served on its own; melted on top of grilled meat, fish or vegetables; used to finish a sauce; or, in this case, stuffed under the skin of poultry. Think herbs, spices, zests, chopped anchovies, capers, spicy condiments and hot chilies.
- Since butter freezes so well, make a batch of compound butter, form it into a log, wrap it in plastic wrap and freeze. Slice off coins when needed.

COOL FACT: LET THE MEAT REST FOR GOD'S SAKE

Have you heard of the term "carry-over cooking"? This is one of the reasons why we let meat rest before slicing into it. The internal temperature of dense foods, like meat, will increase 5–20°F (depending on its size) as it continues to cook when removed from the oven. I like to take my chicken breasts out of the oven at 160°F (71°C) and then let them rest for at least 5 minutes, so they are perfectly cooked to 165°F (74°C).

(NF, LS)

SALMON, LEEK AND CHARD WELLINGTON

When I host a dinner party I try to make as much food ahead of time as possible. There's nothing worse than trying to assemble, cook and serve everything as your guests are arriving. My Salmon, Leek and Chard Wellington is perfect for entertaining for all the right reasons. It's elegant, loaded with flavour and, if you're like me, you'll have it prepped and waiting in the fridge hours before anyone is ringing your doorbell.

MAKES 4 servings
PREP TIME 30 minutes
COOK TIME 15–18 minutes
TOTAL TIME 50 minutes

6 Tbsp (90 mL) butter, divided

1 Tbsp (15 mL) olive oil, divided

2 shallots, finely diced

4 cloves garlic, finely diced or puréed

1 bunch Swiss chard, leafy greens only, roughly chopped

Salt to taste

Freshly ground white pepper to taste

3 leeks, light green and whites only, cut in half lengthwise and thinly sliced

3 Tbsp (45 mL) heavy cream (35%)

All-purpose flour, for dusting

1 puff pastry sheet, thawed according to pkg instructions

1 Tbsp (15 mL) ground sumac (see Sumac Tip p. 18)

1 lb (450 g) piece of salmon, skin and bones removed

1 egg, beaten

1. Preheat oven to 425°F (220°C) and line a baking sheet.
2. Preheat a large sauté pan over medium heat and add 3 Tbsp (45 mL) butter and ½ Tbsp (7 mL) olive oil. When the butter starts to foam, sauté shallots with the garlic until softened, about 3 minutes. Add the Swiss chard, toss and season with a pinch of salt and white pepper. Sauté until wilted, then transfer to a bowl to cool. Once cooled, strain off any excess liquid, finely chop and set aside.
3. Melt remaining butter and olive oil in the same skillet over medium heat. Add leeks, season with salt and white pepper and continue to sauté until softened, about 5–7 minutes.
4. Stir in cream and let it reduce for 1 minute, or until the mixture looks more saucy than wet. Remove from heat and set aside to cool.
5. Dust a little flour onto a clean counter and gently unfold or roll out the puff pastry sheet so that it's large enough to fold around the salmon. Prick pastry with a fork a few times, just like you would a pie crust.
6. Spread an even layer of Swiss chard down the middle of the puff pastry so that it is the same width as the piece of salmon. Layer leeks overtop the Swiss chard.

7. Season both sides of the salmon with salt, white pepper and sumac. Place salmon on top of the chard and leeks and fold the pastry around it to enclose. Trim edges of the pastry, if necessary, with a knife; place, seam side down on lined baking sheet.
8. Brush top and sides of the pastry with the egg wash, score top of the pastry 3 times with a knife and sprinkle with a little salt.
9. Bake 16–18 minutes until pastry is puffed and golden brown.
10. Let rest for 5 minutes before portioning.

SAVED MY LIFE: SETTING THE TABLE THE NIGHT BEFORE

I know this sounds crazy, but if I am having a big holiday dinner party I always set the table the night before, with all the cutlery, glasses, etc., to make sure I have everything I need. It also saves time the day of. Another reason for doing this—and this is very strategic—is so my family doesn't dirty up all the good cutlery and glasses a few hours before dinner, leaving me to scramble and wash the forks, again, for our guests.

WELLINGTON TIPS

- I usually serve this wellington with a simple salad dressed with My Classic French Vinaigrette (see p. 31).
- I wanted to preserve the delicate texture of the Swiss chard leaves, so I'm only using the greens here. I like to hold onto the stems and add them into salads, soups or to simply sauté them and serve them as a side. Say that three times fast.

COOL FACT: PUFF PASTRY LOVES TO BE KEPT COLD

Classic puff pastry is said to have 729 layers of flour and butter. The butter, if kept cold and in its solid state, melts quickly when blasted with heat from the oven. This causes steam pockets that form a really puffy pastry.

(GF, NF, LS)

SPATCHCOCK PIRI PIRI CHICKEN

Want to know the fastest way to roast a whole chicken? Spatchcock it.

This simple method, especially good for grilling and barbecues, means to split and flatten a chicken. This way the chicken cooks evenly and the entire surface of the chicken has more direct contact with the heat, so you get tasty crispy skin all over. My favourite part is that you can cook a whole chicken in 30 minutes.

Piri Piri is basically Portuguese hot sauce. I crave this stuff. Spicy, salty, smoky and tangy. In my recipe I use reconstituted dried chilies instead of fresh. I find the flavours more rounded with less of a spicy kick. This marinade is also great served with grilled meat or shrimp.

MAKES enough for 4–6 servings
PREP TIME 15 minutes
COOK TIME 30 minutes
SPECIAL EQUIPMENT NEEDED blender or food processor

PIRI PIRI SAUCE

¼ cup (60 mL) olive oil

1 lemon, juiced

1 Tbsp (15 mL) rice wine vinegar

1 dried long red chili

1 dried smoked chili (such as chipotle, pasilla, ancho or guajillo)

5–6 garlic cloves, smashed

1–2 Tbsp (30 mL) water (optional)

1 Tbsp (15 mL) paprika

1 Tbsp (15 mL) smoked paprika

5 sprigs fresh thyme, leaves picked

1 tsp (5 mL) dried oregano or 2 tsp (10 mL) dried marjoram

1 bay leaf

½–1 tsp (2–5 mL) salt (or to taste)

CHICKEN

3 lb (1.4 kg) chicken, spatchcocked (see Spatchcock Tip below)

1 lemon, cut into wedges, for garnish

2 Tbsp (30 mL) chopped parsley, for garnish

1. In a small saucepot, combine the olive oil, lemon juice, vinegar, chilies and garlic. Bring to a simmer. Turn off heat and let the dried chilies reconstitute for 10 minutes. Add 1–2 Tbsp (15–30 mL) water if needed.
2. Combine this and the remaining sauce ingredients in a blender or food processor and purée until the dried chilies and bay leaf have broken up, about 3 minutes. Taste and adjust seasoning by adding ½–1 tsp (2–5 mL) salt.
3. Reserve a quarter of the piri piri sauce for basting and rub remaining sauce all over the chicken. Most importantly, rub marinade under the skin of the breasts and legs. Marinate at least 1 hour or up to 1 day ahead in the fridge in a resealable plastic bag.
4. Preheat oven or barbecue to 375°F (190°C). Season marinated chicken lightly with salt and roast about 30 minutes or until the internal temperature is 160°F (71°C), basting halfway through cooking time with the reserved piri piri. Serve with lemon wedges and chopped parsley.

SPATCHCOCK TIP

- The easiest way to spatchcock a chicken is to let your butcher do it for you. If you're doing it on your own with a sharp knife or, even better, a pair of kitchen shears, cut out the backbone of the chicken, starting at the thigh end. Flip the chicken over, breast side up, and flatten it out. Use your hands and body weight on the breastbone. You should hear a few bones cracking. Save the backbone for stock.

(LS)

CURRIED SPINACH AND CHARD PHYLLO PIE

One night, I just couldn't decide between Indian and Greek. I had a big bunch of spinach and Swiss chard that I needed to use up, some feta in the cheese drawer and then I thought . . . spanakopita! To cure my craving for Indian, I added a kick of curry, garam masala and coconut milk into the mix. This pie is packed with healthy greens, warming spices, salty feta and walnuts, all wrapped in layers of flaky phyllo.

Not overpowering or heavy, it makes for a great vegetarian main and is a nice change from the classic.

PREP TIME 25 minutes
COOK TIME 35–40 minutes
REST TIME 10 minutes
SPECIAL EQUIPMENT NEEDED pie plate, pastry brush

- ⅓ cup (80 mL) melted coconut oil or olive oil, for brushing phyllo sheets
- 1 lb (450 g) fresh or frozen Swiss chard (about 1 bunch)
- 1 lb (450 g) fresh or frozen spinach (about 1 bunch)
- 1–2 Tbsp (15–30 mL) coconut oil
- 2 medium onions, finely diced
- 1 clove garlic, puréed
- ½ cup (125 mL) diced celery or fennel bulb
- ¼ tsp (1 mL) ground or freshly grated nutmeg
- 2 tsp (10 mL) curry powder
- 1 tsp (5 mL) garam masala
- Salt to taste
- Pepper to taste
- 2 eggs
- ½ cup (125 mL) coconut milk
- ½ cup (125 mL) chopped walnuts or walnut pieces
- ½ lb (250 g) feta, broken into small pieces
- 1–2 Tbsp (15–30 mL) chopped fresh parsley (optional)
- 10 sheets phyllo, thawed according to pkg instructions

1. Preheat oven to 350°F (175°C) and brush a pie plate with the melted coconut oil or olive oil. Start boiling a large pot of salted water.
2. If using fresh chard, separate stems from leaves, finely chop stems and set aside to sauté with the onions. If using fresh chard and spinach make sure they are washed well since these types of greens can be very sandy.
3. In a large pot of boiling salted water, boil the spinach and chard until wilted, about 2 minutes. Drain in a colander and run under cold water in the sink to cool. Use your hands to give the greens a good squeeze, releasing excess moisture. Finely chop and set aside in a large bowl.
4. In a medium sauté pan over medium heat, add 1 Tbsp (15 mL) coconut oil and sauté onions until translucent, about 3 minutes. Add the garlic, celery, chard stems (if using) and spices and season with salt and pepper. Sauté until softened, about 5 minutes.
5. In the meantime whisk eggs with the coconut milk in a small bowl; set aside.
6. Add sautéed veggies to the spinach and chard, along with the walnuts, feta and parsley. Taste and adjust seasoning if necessary. Let cool slightly, then stir in the coconut milk and egg mixture.
7. While cooling, prepare a pie plate with phyllo crust. Gently brush each sheet of phyllo with melted coconut oil as you go. Layer in pie plate by crisscrossing sheets on top of one another. Leave overhang to wrap around the filling afterwards.
8. Add filling into the phyllo crust and fold the overhang overtop, leaving it ruffled in appearance. Brush the outer layer lightly with oil.
9. Bake 35–40 minutes. If the top is browning too quickly, lightly place a layer of foil overtop. Let rest 10 minutes before serving.

PHYLLO TIPS

- It is very rare I use a whole package of phyllo. You have to thaw out the whole darn package when you use it though, so chances are you will probably have leftover phyllo. Roll up leftover sheets in plastic wrap and store in the fridge for up to a week.
- Phyllo sheets tear easily but don't panic, keep going. In the end it will all look great.
- Sheets also dry out quickly, so keep the stack of sheets covered with a slightly damp cloth while you work.

THEME NIGHTS

It's difficult to pull together the perfect main, the perfect side and the perfect vegetable at the same time. Sometimes it's easier to just pick a theme and go with it—it takes the guesswork out of dinner.

Yes it sounds cheesy, but if you can get over yourself and commit, it can be a heck of a lot of fun. Even if it's just once a month, or a few times a year, it starts a tradition and gives everybody something to look forward to. Simple taco nights, make-your-own pizza dinners or having certain meals in rotation will give you piece of mind when driving home thinking "What the hell am I cooking for dinner? Oh I know, its pizza night!" Perfect.

PIEROGI PARTY

You can buy frozen pierogies in the grocery store anytime, but having an official friends and family pierogi night is a whole lot of fun. You can stuff them with just about anything—meat, veggies, cheese, fruit fillings, the possibilities are endless. Nobody can resist homemade pierogies sautéed in butter, and pierogi dough takes minutes to make with the aid of a food processor. The combination of spelt and all-purpose flour give the dough a slightly nutty quality. It rolls out easily and its elasticity makes it very forgiving, which really helps when working with kids.

(NF)

PIEROGI DOUGH

MAKES twenty-four 3-inch (8 cm) pierogies
PREP TIME 5 minutes
ASSEMBLY TIME 20 minutes
SPECIAL EQUIPMENT NEEDED food processor, 3-inch (8 cm) round cookie cutte

- 1 cup (250 mL) all-purpose flour
- 1 cup (250 mL) spelt flour
- ½ tsp (2 mL) salt
- ¼ cup (60 mL) cold butter, cubed
- 1 egg, lightly beaten
- ½ cup (125 mL) plain yogurt
- Pierogi filling (see p. 124)

1. In a food processor, pulse together the flours with the salt.
2. Add in butter and pulse a few times until cut into pea-sized pieces.
3. Add remaining ingredients and continue to pulse until dough comes together in a ball, about 2 minutes.
4. Transfer dough onto a floured surface and knead into a smooth ball. If the dough feels sticky to the touch, knead in a little more flour. Divide into 2 flattened rounds. Wrap with plastic wrap and place in the refrigerator for 30 minutes to rest. Dough can stay in the fridge like this for up to 2 days.
5. Working one round at a time (keeping the other round in the fridge) roll out the dough ⅛ inch (3 mm) thick on a lightly floured surface. Punch out circles with a cookie cutter or the rim of a glass and proceed to fill with a rounded teaspoon of filling. With fingers, wrap dough around the filling and seal edges. Dough should self-seal when pinched but use a dab of water if necessary. Crimp edges with a fork if you like. Scraps are easy to reroll, just knead them up and pop dough back in the fridge to chill for 10 minutes before rerolling. Dough is easier to roll when chilled.
6. Cook pierogies in boiling salted water until they float to the top; strain then sauté in a hot sauté pan with melted butter. You can also bake at 400°F (200°C) on a lined baking sheet for 5 minutes per side.

SAVED MY LIFE: SPELT FLOUR

I started using spelt flour years ago when I was looking for a tastier replacement for whole wheat. I fell in love with its nutty flavour and was surprised at how easy it is to substitute into recipes. Try replacing 50 percent of your all-purpose flour in a recipe with spelt. It is milder, sweeter and more nutritious than whole wheat. It is not gluten-free though, which is why it is so easy to incorporate into recipes without compromising texture. You can find it now in almost any bulk food, health or organic section of a grocery store.

PIEROGI TIPS

- Dough can be kept in the fridge for up to 2 days.
- Resist overfilling pierogies or they may explode when cooked.
- Freeze pierogies in a single layer on a baking sheet for 1 hour, then transfer into freezer-safe bags to maximize storage space. Cook the same as you would the ones you buy in the frozen food aisle. Boil from frozen until they float, then sauté in butter or oil until golden brown.

PIEROGI NIGHT CONTINUED . . .

(NF, LS)

POTATO, CHEESE AND CHIVE PIEROGI FILLING

MAKES enough to fill 24 pierogies
PREP TIME 20 minutes
COOK TIME 15 minutes
SPECIAL EQUIPMENT NEEDED potato masher

½ lb (250 g) russet potatoes (about 2), peeled and cubed

2 Tbsp (30 mL) butter

1 cup (250 mL) grated old cheddar cheese

Salt to taste

Pepper to taste

2 Tbsp (30 mL) finely chopped chives

1. Place potatoes in a medium-sized saucepot, adding enough cold salted water to cover by 1 inch (2.5 cm). Bring to simmer until potatoes are tender, about 10–15 minutes, then drain.
2. In a large bowl, mash hot potatoes with the butter, cheddar cheese, salt and pepper.
3. Fold in chives. Let mixture cool before filling pierogies. Place in the fridge to expedite cooling process.

(NF)

APPLE PIE PIEROGI FILLING

MAKES enough to fill 24 pierogies
PREP TIME 10 minutes
COOK TIME 5 minutes

4 Golden Delicious or Granny Smith apples, peeled and cut into small cubes

1 Tbsp (15 mL) fresh lemon juice

¼ cup (60 mL) water, divided

2 tsp (10 mL) lemon zest

1-inch (2.5 cm) knob fresh ginger, grated (about 1 Tbsp/15 mL)

⅓ cup (80 mL) cane sugar or honey

½ tsp (2 mL) ground cinnamon

¼ tsp (1 mL) fresh grated nutmeg

Pinch of salt

1 Tbsp (15 mL) cornstarch

1. Place all ingredients, except cornstarch and 1 Tbsp (15 mL) water, into a saucepot over medium heat. Simmer until apples are tender crisp. Add a splash more water if necessary.
2. Mix cornstarch with 1 Tbsp (15 mL) water to create a slurry, then pour into the apple mixture while stirring and bring to a boil; mixture will thicken. Transfer filling to a bowl and let cool before filling pierogies. Place in the fridge to expedite the cooling process.
3. Leftover filling can be used anywhere you may want some apple-pie flavour, such as in yogurt or alongside pancakes or pork.

FALAFEL NIGHT

Falafel Night is one of my favourite theme meals. It's fun to eat and because there is such a variety of flavour and texture, you feel like your tastebuds are going on a trip around the world! The tanginess of the tabbouleh balances the richness of the falafel and the creaminess of the tahini sauce. I love this combination; it's fresh, flavourful and satisfying!

Falafel night is also great for entertaining. Middle Eastern food is often served mezze style, which is a bunch of small plates, dips and salads. Everything can be made ahead of time and served at room temperature, which takes the stress out of hosting a big party. I like to set everything out on a table before my guests arrive so that when they do I don't have to worry about a thing.

There are also a few little extras I like to add, in addition to the pita bread (which I think is mandatory). You don't have to add all of these, you can just pick and choose your favourites: stuffed grape leaves, thinly sliced radishes, carrots, olives, feta cheese, roasted red peppers or a side of fresh vegetables like cucumber, cherry tomatoes, red onion slices and a handful of parsley for good measure.

(GF, NF, LS)

TAHINI YOGURT DIPPING SAUCE

TOTAL TIME 5 minutes

⅔ cup (160 mL) plain yogurt

3 Tbsp (45 mL) tahini

2 Tbsp (30 mL) lemon juice

⅛ tsp (0.5 mL) cayenne (or to taste)

1 Tbsp (15 mL) chopped parsley and/or cilantro

Pinch of salt

1. In a bowl, stir together all ingredients until combined. Taste and adjust seasoning.

FALAFEL NIGHT CONTINUED . . .

(V, GF, NF, LS)

FALAFELS

MAKES 18 falafel patties
PREP TIME 12 hours
COOK TIME 10–15 minutes
SPECIAL EQUIPMENT NEEDED food processor, lunch containers

- 1 cup (250 mL) dried chickpeas, soaked overnight
- 1 cup (250 mL) roughly chopped onion (about 1 onion)
- 2 cloves garlic, peeled
- 2 Tbsp (30 mL) chopped fresh parsley
- 2 Tbsp (30 mL) chopped fresh cilantro
- 1 Tbsp (15 mL) ground cumin
- 2 tsp (10 mL) ground coriander
- ½ tsp (2 mL) chili or cayenne powder
- 2 tsp (10 mL) salt (or to taste)
- 2 tsp (10 mL) baking powder
- 1–2 Tbsp (15–30 mL) lemon juice (or to taste)
- ¼ cup (60 mL) hemp hearts or sesame seeds
- 3–4 Tbsp (45–60 mL) neutral-flavoured oil

1. Drain chickpeas well. In a food processor, pulse together the chickpeas, onion, garlic, parsley and cilantro, about 30 seconds.
2. Add the spices, salt, baking powder and lemon juice; pulse just until blended, about 2–3 minutes. Scrape down bowl of food processor when needed. Transfer to a bowl and stir in the seeds, taste and adjust seasoning with more salt or lemon.
3. Shape by heaping tablespoons into balls; flatten to ½ inch (1 cm) thickness. Arrange in a single layer on a baking sheet; cover and refrigerate for at least 1 hour. See tip to make ahead up until this point.
4. Pour enough oil into a heavy skillet to coat the bottom of the pan; heat over medium-high heat and fry falafel in batches, turning once, about 4 minutes or until golden. With a slotted spatula or spoon, transfer to a paper towel-lined plate to drain.

FALAFEL TIP

- To make ahead, you can either make up until they are formed into balls and let sit in the refrigerator for up to 12 hours, or cook, cool, cover and refrigerate for up to 24 hours. To reheat, bake on a lined baking sheet in a 350°F (175°C) oven for 10 minutes.

WHAT ABOUT KOREAN?

Korean food philosophy is based on the principle of balance between opposites, which is represented through dishes with distinct flavours, colours and textures. Korean food isn't only delicious, it's also incredibly beautiful, which is why it's such a great theme for entertaining and one of my favourite cuisines.

When I'm planning a themed meal, I like to pick one main dish that's the star of the show, which in this case happens to be my Boston Bibb Beef Bulgogi Cups (try saying that ten times fast!).

I started making bulgogi when my kids were small. They both loved beef and I was getting tired of making the same old stews, steaks and tacos, so I started to think "outside the box." The sweetness of the pear, the citrusy burst from the orange and the tenderness of the beef come together in perfect flavour harmony, which is why the kids love it just as much as I do! It's also incredibly quick to throw together, which is ideal for busy weeknights.

I like to serve a bunch of smaller sides or "banchan" in Korean, which are traditionally served alongside almost every meal. One of the most famous is kimchi—a fermented vegetable dish that is both spicy and sour. It's Korea's national dish and the perfect accompaniment to this meal. I love using my sauerkraut recipe (see p. 28), but if you want to keep it traditional, buy a jar of kimchi at the grocery store. My Veggie Glass Noodles and Sweet and Sour Mango Salad are fresh and cooling served alongside the bulgogi. Finish this meal off simply with a bunch of frozen lychees (which are super fun to eat) or thick slices of ripe juicy mango. Remember, it's all about balance!

(V, GF, NF, LS)

VEGGIE GLASS NOODLES

MAKES 4–6 servings
PREP TIME 10 minutes
COOK TIME 10 minutes

- 2½ oz (75 g) dried rice stick noodles (gluten-free)
- 1 Tbsp (15 mL) sesame oil
- 2 Tbsp (30 mL) tamari or soy sauce
- 1 Tbsp (15 mL) maple syrup
- 1 Tbsp (15 mL) rice wine vinegar
- 3 green onions, thinly sliced
- ½ clove garlic, puréed
- 1 Tbsp (15 mL) sesame seeds
- 1 Tbsp (15 mL) neutral-flavoured oil
- ½ onion, thinly sliced
- 1 carrot, cut into thin matchsticks (about 2 inches/5 cm in length)
- ½ red pepper, thinly sliced

1. Cook noodles in boiling salted water according to the package instructions, typically 6–7 minutes. Rinse well in a colander with cool water until cool to the touch. Drain well. Transfer to a serving bowl. Toss immediately with sesame oil to prevent sticking
2. In a small bowl, stir together the tamari (or soy) sauce, maple syrup, vinegar, onions, garlic and sesame seeds. Pour over noodles and toss to coat.
3. Preheat a sauté pan over high heat, add neutral-flavoured oil and onions. Sauté for 1 minute then add remaining ingredients. Sauté for an additional 2–3 minutes until just tender. Toss with noodles and serve.

WHAT ABOUT KOREAN? CONTINUED . . .

BOSTON BIBB BEEF BULGOGI CUPS (P. 130)

(GF, NF, LS)

BOSTON BIBB BEEF BULGOGI CUPS

MAKES 4 servings
PREP TIME 15 minutes
MARINATE TIME at least 3 hours or up to 1 day ahead
COOK TIME 5–10 minutes
SPECIAL EQUIPMENT NEEDED grater or microplane

MARINADE

1 orange, zested

½ orange, juiced

1 Asian pear, grated (can use any pear or even an apple)

2 Tbsp (30 mL) unseasoned rice vinegar

2 Tbsp (30 mL) honey or maple syrup

¼ cup (60 mL) tamari or soy sauce

1 Tbsp (15 mL) sesame oil

4 cloves garlic, puréed

1-inch (2.5 cm) piece ginger, grated (about 1 Tbsp/15 mL)

½ onion, grated or 4 green onions, finely chopped

1 tsp (5 mL) freshly grated white or black pepper

BEEF BULGOGI CUPS

1½ lb (700 g) marinated steak (sirloin, flank or skirt) or bavette, thinly sliced against the grain

2 Tbsp (30 mL) neutral-flavoured oil

1 head Boston bibb lettuce, separated into lettuce cups for wraps

GARNISHES

1–2 Tbsp (15–30 mL) sesame seeds

3 green onions, thinly sliced

2–4 Tbsp (30–60 mL) chopped cilantro

4 radishes, thinly sliced

Cheap and Simple Sauerkraut (see p. 28) or 1 jar of Kimchi

Homemade Hot Sauce (see p. 25)

1. In a bowl, mix together all ingredients for the marinade. Marinate sliced beef for at least 3 hours or up to 1 day ahead in a resealable plastic bag or sealed container.
2. In a large skillet over medium-high heat, add 1–2 Tbsp (30 mL) oil and cook beef with marinade until just cooked through, about 5 minutes. Depending on the size of your pan you may have to do this in batches. Traditionally the beef in bulgogi is not seared, so don't worry about getting a lot of colour on it, which risks overcooking the beef. Beef will release juices and mix with the marinade for an instant sauce that you pour over the bulgogi when serving. Yum.

BULGOGI TIP

- Partially freeze meat for about 15 minutes before slicing. It will help you get the strips nice and thin, especially if you don't have a super sharp knife.

(NF, GF, V)

SWEET AND SOUR MANGO SALAD

MAKES 4 side servings
TOTAL TIME 10 minutes

2 Tbsp (30 mL) fresh lime juice

1 tsp (5 mL) lime zest

1 Tbsp (15 mL) maple syrup or honey

1 Tbsp (15 mL) fish sauce (or soy sauce, if vegetarian)

1 bird's eye chili, finely chopped or ½ tsp (2 mL) chili flakes (or to taste)

1 Tbsp (15 mL) sesame oil

1 firm unripe (hard) mango (about 1 lb/450 g)

1 red pepper, thinly sliced

1 shallot, thinly sliced

Salt to taste

2 Tbsp (30 mL) chopped basil (Thai basil if you have it) and/or cilantro

⅓ cup (80 mL) coarsely chopped cashews, peanuts or sesame seeds

1. In a large bowl, whisk together a simple dressing of lime juice, zest, honey or maple syrup, fish sauce, chili and sesame oil.
2. Cut the bottom and top end off the mango. Place mango on flattened ends to help peel with a knife. Cut into thin slices and stack to cut into thin strips.
3. Add mango, pepper, shallot, basil and/or cilantro to the dressing and toss. Taste and adjust seasoning with salt.
4. Sprinkle chopped nuts or seeds overtop.

SPANISH FIESTA

The great thing about paella is that it's the quintessential one-pot wonder. Grab a good baguette, some manchego cheese and Spanish ham. Open an inexpensive bottle of good Spanish wine and finish this meal with my simple Vanilla Bean Pudding (see p. 170).

(GF, NF, LS)

CHICKEN AND CHORIZO PAELLA

MAKES 6–8 servings
PREP TIME 25 minutes
COOK TIME 30 minutes
SPECIAL EQUIPMENT NEEDED large cast-iron or heavy-bottomed sauté pan

5 cups (1.25 L) chicken stock

¼ tsp (1 mL) saffron threads (about 1 small pinch)

1 lb (450 g) boneless skinless chicken thighs (about 4), quartered

Salt to taste

Pepper to taste

2 Tbsp (30 mL) olive oil, divided

¼ lb (125 g) dry-cured chorizo sausage, cubed

1 onion, preferably Spanish, diced

2 cloves garlic, minced

1 large tomato, diced

1 red bell pepper, finely diced

1 cup (250 mL) diced zucchini

½ Tbsp (7 mL) paprika

1 tsp (5 mL) smoked paprika

1 Tbsp (15 mL) fresh thyme leaves

1 cup (250 mL) bomba, calasparra, arborio or any other medium-grain rice

½ cup (125 mL) dry white wine

½ cup (125 mL) fresh or thawed frozen peas

2 Tbsp (30 mL) minced parsley, for garnish

2 lemons, quartered, for garnish

1. In a saucepot, heat stock to a boil, cover and keep hot over low heat.
2. Measure out 1 cup (250 mL) hot stock and stir in the saffron to steep; set aside.
3. Season chicken with salt and pepper. Preheat a pan over high heat; add 1 Tbsp (15 mL) olive oil and brown chicken. Transfer to a plate.
4. Lower heat to medium. In the same pan, add the remaining oil and brown chorizo, about 5 minutes. Transfer to a plate.
5. In the same dirty pan with the chorizo-flavoured oil, sauté onion until softened, about 3 minutes. Stir in garlic and sauté until softened, about 2 minutes.
6. Add diced tomato, red pepper and zucchini to the pan and sauté to soften slightly, about 5 minutes. Season with salt and stir in paprika, smoked paprika and fresh thyme.
7. Stir in rice and sauté for 1 minute.
8. Stir in white wine until absorbed.
9. Ladle in ½ cup (125 mL) stock and stir until the rice has absorbed it.
10. Ladle in another 1 cup (250 mL) stock, spread all ingredients in a single, even layer and let simmer, undisturbed, until liquid is absorbed. No more stirring.
11. Once stock is absorbed, pour the reserved saffron broth over the rice. Nestle chicken into rice and sprinkle the chorizo overtop. Continue to simmer until rice is tender and no liquid remains, tasting along the way, about 10 minutes. If you taste the rice and it is still undercooked, add in more stock and continue to simmer.

12. Sprinkle peas overtop towards the end to warm through. Rice should be almost crispy on the edges of pan and soft and fluffy in the middle. Garnish with parsley and lemon wedges and serve tableside right out of the pot.

PAELLA TIPS

- For a seafood version, use fish stock and replace 1 lb (450 g) chicken with 1 lb (450 g) seafood of choice. Seafood is also an easy addition since it cooks so quickly, no need to brown it first like the chicken. Just make sure it's in bite-sized pieces and toss it in halfway through cook time.
- Have leftover gravy? Add this to your stock for major flavour.

COOL FACT: WHY SAFFRON IS EXPENSIVE

Saffron is the dried stigma strands from crocus flowers. They have to be handpicked, then dried, and each flower yields only three strands. You need to harvest a lot of crocuses to make a small amount of saffron. The good thing is that very little makes a large impact in a recipe.

THAI IT UP

My food cravings are typically what drive my eating habits. When you think "food cravings" you kinda think of "bad" food. Yeah, I crave chocolate, wine and coffee, but I also hunger for the nostalgic comfort that comes with a simple roast chicken dinner or—one of my all-time favourites—getting all hopped up on a truly great spicy curry. I like to believe that this is my food intuition kicking in. So, let's just embrace it.

Thai food is known for its balance of bold flavours. It is also known for its lack of actual recipes and measurements. It's all about taste. Traditional Thai family recipes are passed down without the need for measuring spoons, so here is a great opportunity to have fun with the measurements. The fresh herbs, the creamy curries, that slightly bitter flavour offset with sweetness and spice—need I say more?

Thai dishes are typically served with rice (see Coconut Rice p. 94) or use whatever you have on hand. I really would love for you to try making a homemade Thai Curry Paste (see p. 135) for a truly authentic experience. Also, if you want to throw in another dish for Thai-ing up your evening, try my Wrap-it-Up Fresh Spring Rolls recipe (see p. 136).

(GF, NF, LS)

SHRIMP AND GREEN BEAN CURRY

MAKES 4 servings
MARINATE TIME 20 minutes
COOK TIME 20 minutes

- 1 lb (450 g) peeled raw medium or large shrimp
- 1 tsp (5 mL) ground cumin
- 1 tsp (5 mL) ground coriander
- 2 tsp (10 mL) turmeric
- Pinch of salt
- 2 Tbsp (30 mL) coconut oil
- 1 large onion, diced
- 2 Tbsp (30 mL) Thai curry paste (recipe follows) or store-bought curry paste
- 1 tsp (5 mL) ground cardamom
- One 400-mL (13.5 fl oz) can coconut milk
- 1 carrot, thinly sliced
- 10 oz (300 g) green beans, trimmed and cut into 1-inch (2.5 cm) pieces
- 1 red pepper, chopped
- 2 Tbsp (30 mL) chopped fresh cilantro
- Salt to taste (optional)
- Pepper to taste (optional)
- Lime wedges, for garnish

1. In a bowl, toss shrimp with the cumin, coriander, turmeric and salt and let marinate for at least 20 minutes.
2. In a large saucepot over medium heat, add oil and sauté onion until softened, about 5 minutes. Stir in the curry paste and cardamom and cook for an additional 2–3 minutes to let the spices come to life.
3. Add in coconut milk and bring to a simmer.
4. Add carrot and green beans and simmer, covered, about 5 minutes or until tender crisp.
5. Add in red pepper and shrimp and simmer for an additional 3–5 minutes, or until shrimp are cooked through.
6. Taste and add seasonings if necessary. Serve over rice with a squeeze of fresh lime juice.

STORE-BOUGHT CURRY PASTE TIP

- Those small bottles of store-bought curry paste are great to use in a pinch, but I have always found they taste wishy-washy. They lack the bold and fresh flavours Thai food is so well known for.
- If you are going to use store-bought paste, try sautéing 2 cloves of crushed garlic and 2 tsp (10 mL) chopped fresh ginger with the onions for an additional flavour boost. Don't hesitate to taste your curry during the cooking process and add an extra pinch of cumin, coriander or a few chili flakes if you want.

(GF, NF, LS)

THAI CURRY PASTE (NAM PRIK GAENG KIEW WAN)

MAKES ½ cup (125 mL)
COOK TIME 15 minutes
SPECIAL EQUIPMENT NEEDED food processor or mortar and pestle

- 1 Tbsp (15 mL) coriander seeds, toasted
- 1 Tbsp (15 mL) cumin seeds, toasted
- 10 peppercorns, toasted
- 4 bird's eye chilies, red or green, roughly chopped
- 3 Tbsp (45 mL) chopped shallots
- 4 cloves garlic, roughly chopped
- 1 tsp (5 mL) grated galangal or ginger
- 1 Tbsp (15 mL) chopped lemongrass
- ½ lime, zested
- 6 dried or 3 fresh kaffir lime leaves
- 1 tsp (5 mL) salted shrimp paste or anchovy paste
- 1 tsp (5 mL) peeled chopped fresh turmeric or ground turmeric
- 1 tsp (5 mL) salt

1. Add all ingredients to a food processor and pulse until a paste forms. This takes only a few minutes. If using a mortar and pestle, grind toasted seeds and peppercorns first then add in the remaining ingredients, bashing everything around until you have a paste—this could take up to 30 minutes.
2. Label, date and refrigerate for up to 3 weeks, or freeze for up to 3 months.
3. To use in recipes, fry ¼ cup (60 mL) paste over medium heat until browned, about 3 minutes, then continue on with the recipe.

SAVED MY LIFE: FINDING A FEW GOOD ETHNIC FOOD MARKETS IN MY NEIGHBOURHOOD

If you have one already, great! If you don't, start exploring. When my kids were younger (like before they got cool and were not embarrassed to be seen hanging with their mom) they loved to check out ethnic markets, picking out things they had never seen before to try.

THAI CURRY TIPS

- Lime leaves and fresh turmeric are items I buy in very small quantities and keep frozen until needed.
- Fresh turmeric is a little tricky to work with. The first time I bought it, I was adding it to my smoothies and it stained everything it touched. Grate it off from the root directly into a bowl when you want it instead of trying to chop it.
- This curry paste recipe was given to me by my good friend and best high school teacher ever, Jill Mortenson. Jill says that she makes two different versions of this for her family. She uses one Thai chili for a mild kid-friendly curry and another with more for herself.

COOL FACT: GALANGAL AND KAFFIR LIME LEAVES ARE GREAT FOR EXPERIMENTING WITH

Galangal and ginger look very similar. How are they different? Galangal is woodier, not as juicy and harder to grate. It also has more of a kick than ginger. It has been described also as being piney or citrusy.

Kaffir lime leaves are dark green, thick and glossy. You can buy these leaves dried, but they are less flavourful so use double the amount called for in a recipe when dried.

THAI IT UP CONTINUED . . .

(V, GF, NF, LS)

WRAP-IT-UP FRESH SPRING ROLLS

MAKES 8 spring rolls
PREP TIME 10 minutes
COOK TIME 5 minutes
WRAP TIME 10 minutes

2 cups (500 mL) rice vermicelli noodles or other leftover Asian noodles

Asian Dipping Sauce (see below)

10 oz (300 g) cooked chicken or turkey, cut into thin strips

½ red pepper, thinly sliced

¼ cucumber, quartered lengthwise, seeds removed and cut into thin strips

1 carrot, peeled and cut into matchsticks

½ mango, peeled and thinly sliced

⅓ cup (80 mL) fresh basil, cilantro or mint leaves

8½-inch (22 cm) diameter rice paper wrappers

ASIAN DIPPING SAUCE

3 Tbsp (45 mL) rice wine vinegar

2 tsp (10 mL) toasted sesame oil

2 Tbsp (30 mL) tamari or soy sauce

1 tsp (5 mL) maple syrup or honey

1 green onion, finely chopped

½ clove garlic, puréed

1 tsp (5 mL) Sriracha or your favourite hot sauce (optional)

1. Cook noodles according to package instructions. Drain well and set aside to cool in a medium-sized bowl. (If doing this ahead of time, drizzle with a little oil to prevent noodles from sticking.)
2. Make the Asian Dipping Sauce in a small bowl. Whisk together all ingredients and, if you like a little heat, add in your favourite hot sauce. Use as a dipping sauce or toss with the noodles.
3. Have everything in its place (mise en place) and ready to go. Cut all vegetables and chicken before assembling. Fill a medium sauté pan with 1 inch (2.5 cm) water and heat on the stovetop until very warm. You want it hot enough to soften the rice wrappers but not so hot you can't put your fingers in it.
4. Dampen a clean tea towel and place on the counter. With your fingers, dip 1 wrapper into hot water and rotate the wrapper in water until softened, about 3 seconds. Gently lay wrapper flat on the damp tea towel and start placing your fillings horizontally in a row across the centre, leaving 2 inches (5 cm) along the top and bottom and 1 inch (2.5 cm) on each side. Try not to overstuff with noodles and make room for more of the "good" stuff, like all the veggie strips. Add a few basil or cilantro leaves. Roll from the bottom up, tucking in edges halfway through. The aim is to make a nice tight roll; repeat with remaining rolls. If not eaten right away, store in an airtight container with a slightly damp paper towel between layers to prevent sticking and drying out. These can be made up to 8 hours ahead of time and can be wrapped individually in plastic wrap for lunches.

SPRING ROLL TIPS

- These easy-to-use, paper-thin, woven-looking rice paper wrappers make any food bundled inside quite charming. Healthy, kid friendly and gluten and peanut-free, they are a perfect solution for guilt-free school lunches, quick weeknight dinners or party trays. If you have any leftover protein and a few vegetables kicking around the fridge you can rice paper–wrap yourself a meal in minutes.
- Vegetarian? Pescatarian? Try adding extra veggies, thin strips of your favourite firm tofu or tempeh or a few previously cooked shrimp to each wrap instead of the chicken or turkey.
- Rice paper wrappers can be found in the Asian food aisle of any grocer, but for more varieties of shapes, sizes and brands go to a Vietnamese or Chinese market. The best ones are those made with only rice or a combination of rice and tapioca starch.
- How to store rice paper? Once opened, store in a resealable plastic bag. They last pretty much forever. Several years!

SAVED MY LIFE: BUYING SOY-FREE SEASONING SAUCES

I get regular requests at work for foods that accommodate specific dietary restrictions. Soy allergies are among them. Tamari sauce is great and readily available but coconut aminos has been my new go-to product to replace soy. Made from the sap of a coconut tree, it is a soy-free seasoning sauce plus it's gluten-free, lower in sodium and vegan. It's not as potent as soy sauce but it works in a pinch.

CAN I HAVE A SNACK?

I should have been more aggressive with rules about in-between meal snacking. Even though I still line the pantry with jars full of healthier food choices like dried fruit, homemade snack mixes, granola and nuts, these things seem to only mildly satiate my kids as they hang off the pantry doors.

It is my own fault. I am a grazer. I would much prefer to have ten small meals a day than three big ones.

Here is a chapter all about snacks—salty, sweet and savoury. Most of them are really good for you!

(V, GF, LS)

SPICED NUTS

Four cups of spiced nuts for a snack may seem like a lot, but you only eat a handful at a time. They make a simply perfect finger nibble as well as being a welcome addition to any appetizer plate, charcuterie board or salad. I love to have a stash of these on hand over the holidays for the occasional friendly pop-in.

MAKES 4 cups (1 L)
PREP TIME 3 minutes
BAKE TIME 8–10 minutes

- 2 Tbsp (30 mL) neutral-flavoured oil
- 2 Tbsp (30 mL) olive oil
- 2 tsp (10 mL) tamari sauce
- 2 tsp (10 mL) paprika
- 1 tsp (5 mL) smoked paprika
- 1 tsp (5 mL) cayenne, chili or Espelette powder
- 2 tsp (10 mL) salt
- Pepper to taste
- 2 cups (500 mL) raw pecans
- 2 cups (500 mL) raw almonds

1. Preheat oven to 350°F (175°C) and line a baking sheet.
2. In a large bowl, whisk together the oils with the tamari, spices, salt and pepper.
3. Add nuts and toss to coat.
4. Transfer to a lined baking sheet and bake 8–10 minutes, tossing halfway through cook time, until aromatic and browned.
5. Let cool completely before storing in an airtight container. Nuts will crisp up further while cooling.

ESPELETTE PEPPER TIP

- Espelette (or Piment d'Espelette) is a French chili pepper known for its use in Basque-style cooking. It can be found in most specialty food stores. The peppers are considered rare, so they are pricey but a really nice treat. The heat is moderate compared to other chili powders.

(V, GF, NF, LS)

BABA GANOUSH

Eggplant is not something I buy all the time; however, it is one of those things I crave. Every now and then I just need to have eggplant Parmesan or baba ganoush. I love making a big batch of this smoky, luscious Mediterranean dip around the holidays when company is abundant. This recipe does make a large batch, so feel free to half the recipe.

Eggplants come in different shapes and sizes, so use whatever is on hand. I like the baby ones, since they roast faster. I also find smaller eggplants release less water when cooked.

MAKES 3 cups (750 mL)
PREP TIME 5 minutes
COOK TIME 30–60 minutes
SPECIAL EQUIPMENT NEEDED food processor

- 2 lb (700 g) eggplant (the smaller ones roast faster)
- 2 Tbsp (30 mL) tahini
- ½–1 clove garlic, puréed
- 3–4 Tbsp (45–60 mL) fresh lemon juice (or to taste)
- 2 Tbsp (30 mL) extra virgin olive oil
- Salt to taste
- 1 tsp (5 mL) smoked paprika (optional)

1. Preheat oven to broil, or medium-high if using a barbecue (or grill).
2. Prick eggplant all over with a fork to allow liquid and steam to escape. Place on a foil-lined baking sheet if broiling, or place directly on the grill for barbecuing. Eggplant will take about 30 minutes, depending on size, until tender with a charred skin. You want to be able to pierce the flesh easily with a fork.
3. Once cooked, transfer eggplant into a colander fit over a bowl; drain and cool completely before removing the skin.
4. Scrape all flesh from the eggplant, discard any liquid that has drained and transfer to a food processor along with the remaining ingredients. I suggest starting with half of a clove of garlic and 3 Tbsp (45 mL) lemon juice; add more if needed after tasting.
5. Purée to desired consistency—I like mine a little chunky.

BABA GANOUSH TIP

- Larger eggplants will release more water than smaller ones, so make sure to let them drain in a colander to avoid a watery baba ganoush.

(V, GF, NF, LS)

GUACAMOLE

Did you know that avocados are hard to come by around Super Bowl season? The demand for guacamole is so great that most suppliers are in short supply and increase their price. These are the kinds of things you learn when working day-in day-out as a chef in a restaurant, and it's a little known fact handed down to me by my great friend Head Chef Jason Cox of Opus.

We make some version of guacamole every week. Sometimes it's my daughter just smashing an avocado with a fork, sprinkling salt and pepper and squeezing fresh lime on top until it satisfies her palate, other times it's my recipe below. Both are equally satisfying.

MAKES 2 cups (500 mL)
COOK TIME 10 minutes

1 Tbsp (15 mL) freshly squeezed lime juice (approx.)

2 Tbsp (30 mL) finely diced onion

½ tsp (2 mL) ground cumin

½ clove garlic, puréed

½ jalapeno, seeds and ribs removed, finely diced

2 ripe avocados

½ tsp (2 mL) salt (or to taste)

Freshly ground black pepper to taste

1 Tbsp (15 mL) chopped cilantro

1. In a medium-sized bowl, add all ingredients except cilantro and smash with a fork to desired consistency.
2. Stir in cilantro. Taste and adjust seasoning with salt, pepper and lime juice.
3. To prevent oxidization, store in the fridge with plastic wrap touching the surface of the guacamole for up to 3 days. Another option is adding a thin layer of water over the entire surface. Pour off the water and stir before serving.

AVOCADO TIPS

- Avocados do not begin to soften until after they are picked from the tree and they are usually put on the shelf hard. So basically, it's pure luck if you need ripe avocados the day of and can find them. When buying avocados I typically buy unripe ones knowing they will ripen in the next day or two, rather than buying ripe ones that will end up in the garbage if not eaten immediately.
- How to choose a ripe avocado? The riper an avocado is the darker green its skin. It should yield to a firm but gentle pressure but not be mushy.
- How to get avocados to ripen faster? Put them in a paper bag in the warmest place possible, like a windowsill or close to your oven. Adding another overripe fruit, like a banana, will also help. They still may take up to two days to ripen.

COOL FACT: HOW TO PREVENT OXIDATION AND DISCOLOURATION IN FRUITS AND VEGETABLES

You can create a barrier from the air by covering what you want protected in plastic wrap, water or even sometimes oil.

You can also use some type of acid. I always keep citric acid in my food-styling kit and mix it with water to cover certain fruits and vegetables, keeping them perfect until ready to shoot. Apples, avocados and artichokes all brown and discolour easily. You can soak cut fruit or vegetables in water with a few tablespoons of lime or lemon juice, vinegar or even a crushed vitamin C tablet—all these will help prevent discolouration until ready to use.

(GF, NF, LS)

BROWN BUTTER AND ROSEMARY POPCORN

My whole teenage life I thought you needed a microwave or popcorn maker to make popcorn. Parents, this may be one of the most valuable techniques to teach your kids: how to pop corn. If you have popcorn kernels in your pantry, you always have access to a cheap and healthy snack.

This is my savoury and slightly more sophisticated version of popcorn that I like to serve at dinner parties along with a meal, at last minute cocktail gatherings or as a snack.

Brown butter and rosemary? I mean, need I say more? Ok, well, if you have never had this flavour combination before think of the bold aromatic pine-like taste of rosemary mixed with buttery nutty caramelized liquid gold, drizzled over popcorn.

MAKES 4 servings
PREP TIME 5 minutes
COOK TIME 10 minutes
SPECIAL EQUIPMENT NEEDED medium saucepot with a lid or popcorn maker

¼ cup (60 mL) butter

1 Tbsp (15 mL) finely chopped fresh rosemary

1–2 Tbsp (22½–30 mL) olive oil

⅓ cup (80 mL) popcorn kernels

Salt to taste

Pepper to taste

1. Melt butter in a small saucepot over medium heat until foamy, about 3 minutes.
2. Add rosemary, increase heat to medium-high and swirl butter in the pot occasionally until you notice little brown specks or browning of butter, about 3 minutes. Remove from heat.
3. Coat bottom of a medium saucepot with a thin layer of olive oil. Sprinkle kernels evenly over the bottom of the pot. Cover with a lid, heat to high and wait until you hear the kernels pop. Turn down heat slightly; popcorn should be done in about 5 minutes. As soon as you hear the popping slow down, remove from heat to prevent burning.
4. Transfer popcorn to a large bowl, pour brown butter and rosemary mixture overtop and toss with salt and pepper to taste.

SAVED MY LIFE: POPCORN IN THE PANTRY

Popcorn is quite possibly the cheapest and, depending on how you make it, healthiest snack food out there. Did you know that popcorn kernels are a different seed than the ones used for corn and all are non-GMO? Yes, even the cheapest brand and your movie theatre popcorn are not genetically modified.

COOL FACT: WHAT REALLY HAPPENS WHEN YOU BROWN BUTTER

As butter melts, water evaporates and milk proteins brown, separating from the liquid. This infuses a nutty, toasty flavour to the brown butter, known as beurre noisette (hazelnut butter).

(NF, LS)

EASY HERBY CHEDDAR CHEESE BISCUITS

If you want to get your kids in the kitchen you need to be strategic when selecting recipes. Kids need to feel that "I-made-this" realization quickly. They also like basic recipes that they can get creative with. This recipe comes from an episode I did hosting Best Recipes Ever on CBC, and my daughter makes it all the time. It's a simple recipe made with pantry staples that teaches kids some basic pastry skills. Also, there is nothing quite like warm biscuits smothered in butter.

MAKES 12 biscuits
PREP TIME 15 minutes
COOK TIME 15 minutes
SPECIAL EQUIPMENT NEEDED box grater

- 1¾ cups (435 mL) spelt or all-purpose flour
- 4 tsp (20 mL) baking powder
- 1½ Tbsp (22 mL) fresh thyme leaves, chopped rosemary or Herbes de Provence (see p. 18)
- ½ tsp (2 mL) salt
- ½ tsp (2 mL) pepper
- ½ tsp (2 mL) garlic powder
- ¼ cup (60 mL) cold butter, coarsely grated with a box grater
- 1 cup (250 mL) shredded old cheddar cheese
- 1 Tbsp (15 mL) maple syrup (optional)
- 1 cup (250 mL) whole milk or buttermilk

1. Preheat oven to 425°F (220°C) and grease or line a baking sheet.
2. In a large bowl, whisk together the flour, baking powder, herbs, salt, pepper and garlic powder.
3. Toss butter and cheese in the flour mixture with hands until evenly distributed. Grated butter and cheese should be coated in flour.
4. If using maple syrup, stir into the milk. Pour milk into the flour mix and stir with a fork until ragged moist dough forms. Get your hands in there as well to give it a quick knead.
5. Using ¼ cup (60 mL) at a time, drop dough onto the baking sheet, spacing biscuits 1½ inches (4 cm) apart. Bake 13–15 minutes, until puffed and lightly golden on top.

BISCUIT TIPS

- For perfectly round or different-sized biscuits, pat or lightly roll out dough on a well-floured surface. Flour round cookie cutters as well to easily punch out biscuits from the dough.
- Make dough ahead of time, cover with plastic wrap and store in the fridge until needed. Bake biscuits just before dinner to enjoy warm, right out of the oven.

COOL FACT: THE EASIEST WAS TO CUT BUTTER OR LARD INTO PASTRY

Using a box grater to cut cold butter into pastry is by far the easiest method. It's way faster than cutting it in with a pastry blender or 2 knives, and you also bypass digging out (and then having to clean) your food processor or stand mixer. It also yields a really flaky pastry. If using lard, I find 10 minutes in the freezer before grating helps. Lard melts faster than butter and grates better when frozen.

(V, GF)

HOMEMADE POWER BARS

Granola bars have come a long way. People want more protein, energy, fortified fibre, full servings of fruits and vegetables and whole-meal replacements in a quick convenient food. All of this can now be found in an individually wrapped bar. Yeah, I buy them from time to time and I have my favourites, but I still like to make my own. I find it less expensive and I can put exactly what I want in them.

These bars, a family favourite, mimic the well-known Larabar food bar. Their sweetness comes solely from dates, which are puréed and make a perfect binder for nuts, seeds, dried fruit and flavour. Try this base recipe to start and then experiment. See tips below for some alternate flavour combinations.

MAKES 10–12 bars, 25 squares or thirty-six 1-inch (2.5 cm) balls
PREP TIME 15 minutes
REST TIME 2 hours or overnight
SPECIAL EQUIPMENT NEEDED food processor

3 cups (750 mL) raw almonds, coarsely ground

⅓ cup (80 mL) sunflower seeds, coarsely ground

⅓ cup (80 mL) ground flax seeds

½ cup (125 mL) sesame seeds

3 cups (750 mL) packed pitted Medjool dates

1 tsp (5 mL) ground cinnamon

Pinch of salt

2 tsp (10 mL) Pure Vanilla Extract (see p. 14)

1 cup (250 mL) chopped dried fruit or shredded coconut (optional)

1. Line a square baking pan with parchment paper (see Cool Fact below).
2. In a medium-sized bowl, combine almonds and seeds.
3. Using a food processor, make date paste by pulsing pitted dates with the cinnamon, salt and vanilla. Paste may form into a ball in the processor. If so, break apart with your hands and continue to pulse.
4. Add nuts and seeds to the processor and continue to pulse, breaking up date paste from time to time until fully incorporated. The date paste is very thick and you may think that all the dry ingredients will not get fully incorporated. They will, it just requires some muscle on your part.
5. Transfer to a lined baking pan. Press paste to form a single, even layer. Fingers, the back of a spoon or a good sturdy spatula can help.
6. Cover with plastic wrap and let firm up in the refrigerator for 2 hours or overnight. Take off binder clips and use parchment handles to lift bars out of the pan. Cut, place in resealable bags and store in the refrigerator. These freeze very well.

POWER BAR TIPS

- Food processors are great for coarsely grinding nuts and seeds in big batches; however, for small batches and spices, I use a cheap coffee grinder for nuts, seeds and spices only.
- For Chocolate Mint Power Bars, add ¼ cup (60 mL) cocoa powder and ½ tsp (2 mL) peppermint extract to the date paste while processing. For Cherry Coconut Power Bars, add ½ cup (125 mL) chopped dried cherries and ½ cup (125 mL) shredded coconut after processing.
- For a nut-free version omit nuts and replace with an equal amount of seeds (like pumpkin seeds).
- For decadent-looking bars, or a great healthy dessert, melt 2–3 oz (60–90 g) white or dark chocolate and drizzle overtop.

COOL FACT: HOW TO GET SQUARES OUT OF THE PAN

To line a baking pan for squares or bars, use 2 cut layers of parchment and crisscross to cover the bottom and sides of the pan. Use binder clips to hold parchment to the sides of the pan. Once the bars are finished baking you can take the binder clips off and lift the bars out of the pan using the parchment handles.

(GF, NF, LS)

INSANELY GOOD BANANA OAT SQUARES

These dense, moist, insanely good oat squares are packed with banana, chocolate and vanilla flavour. They have no gluten, no nuts, ground flax replaces eggs and ripe bananas replace all the sugar. Plus they bake in 15 minutes!

These are perfect for a last minute dessert or your kid's school fundraiser. Skip the chocolate chips and they are officially guilt-free.

MAKES one 9 × 13–inch (23 × 33 cm) baking pan
PREP TIME 15 minutes
COOK TIME 15–20 minutes
SPECIAL EQUIPMENT NEEDED food processor, spice grinder or blender capable of grinding grains

3½ cups (875 mL) large flake oats (gluten-free), ground into flour

½ tsp (2 mL) baking powder

½ tsp (2 mL) baking soda

1 tsp (5 mL) ground cinnamon

½ tsp (2 mL) nutmeg

2 Tbsp (30 mL) ground flax

Pinch of salt

4 ripe bananas

¼ cup (60 mL) milk or unsweetened milk alternative

½ cup (125 mL) yogurt

¼ cup (60 mL) melted butter or coconut oil, cooled slightly

1 Tbsp (15 mL) Pure Vanilla Extract (see p. 14)

1 cup (250 mL) mini chocolate chips

1. Preheat oven to 350°F (175°C). Grease or line a baking pan.
2. Grind oats into oat flour in a food processor, spice grinder or blender, about 30 seconds. Transfer to a large bowl.
3. In the same large bowl, combine remaining dry ingredients.
4. In a blender or food processor, purée bananas with the milk, yogurt, melted butter or coconut oil and vanilla.
5. Pour wet ingredients over dry and stir until combined. Stir in the chocolate chips.
6. Pour into the baking pan and spread batter evenly with the back of a spoon or a small offset spatula.
7. Bake for 15 minutes, or until set.
8. Cool and cut into squares or bars.

COOL FACT: WHY GRIND YOUR OWN FLOUR?

I can't image having the time to grind all my own flours, however people are doing this. This is truly taking whole foods to a whole other level.

Whole grains are always going to be cheaper than those already ground. They are also going to taste better. You can buy stand-alone grain mills or grain mill attachments for stand mixers if this is something you are going to dive into. It is a great idea if your home is gluten-free, and you really need to have complete control over your ingredients. Also, remember to store freshly ground flours in the fridge or freezer if you are not using them within the first few days. They go rancid quickly.

(V, LS)

LEMON SEED AND SPICE LOAF

My spiced up version of this lemon poppy seed loaf is bright, tangy and speckled with a variety of super seeds. A thick slice of this loaf is the perfect companion to afternoon tea. I use coconut oil, nut milk and ground flax to make this vegan. If the mild licorice tones of anise seem too adventurous for you, try ground cardamom. Cardamom will lend a lightly floral fragrance and minty flavour.

Bring this loaf to your next business meeting—food bribery is a powerful tool in the workplace and everyone loves a good lemon loaf.

MAKES 1 loaf
PREP TIME 20 minutes
COOK TIME about 40 minutes

1 cup (250 mL) milk of choice

¾ cup (185 mL) honey, warmed slightly if too thick

½ cup (125 mL) unsweetened applesauce

⅓ cup (80 mL) melted coconut oil + extra for greasing pan

2 tsp (10 mL) Pure Vanilla Extract (see p. 14)

1 lemon, zested and juiced

1 Tbsp (15 mL) ground flax seeds

1 Tbsp (15 mL) ground pumpkin seeds

2 Tbsp (30 mL) chia seeds

2 Tbsp (30 mL) hemp seeds

2 Tbsp (30 mL) sesame seeds

1¾ cups (435 mL) spelt or all-purpose flour

1 tsp (5 mL) baking powder

1 tsp (5 mL) baking soda

¾ tsp (4 mL) ground anise or cardamom

Pinch of salt

1. Preheat oven to 350°F (175°C) and grease pan with coconut oil.
2. In a large bowl, stir together wet ingredients with lemon zest and seeds. Set aside for a few minutes to thicken.
3. In a medium-sized bowl, whisk remaining dry ingredients together.
4. Stir dry into wet ingredients until just combined. Batter will be on the runny side but don't worry.
5. Pour into greased pan and bake 30–40 minutes or until cake tester comes out clean.

SAVED MY LIFE: REPLACING EGGS OR DAIRY

I don't know how many times I have gone to bake something only to find an empty milk or egg carton in the fridge. Having flax or chia seeds in the pantry along with a tetra pack of shelf stable almond milk means that I always have backup. 1 Tbsp (15 mL) of ground chia or flax mixed with 3 Tbsp (45 mL) water can replace 1 egg.

CREAMSICLE COCONUT TRUFFLES
THREE-INGREDIENT NUT BUTTER COOKIES
SUPERNATURAL VEGAN BROWNIES

(GF)

THREE-INGREDIENT NUT BUTTER COOKIES

It's time for peanut butter to wise up and realize there are a bunch of other really delicious nut butters out there that make an amazing (if not better) cookie. Most grocery stores carry the standards: cashew, almond and hazelnut. If you buy in bulk and have a food processor at home it's easy (and cheaper) to make your own nut butter; then you can get crazy with macadamia, pecan or even Brazil nuts (if you're feeling luxurious). I make these cookies often and I'm always switching up the nut butter based on what I have on hand. It's easily adaptable and an easy recipe for kids to make—three ingredients, 15 minutes. Great for little hands and short attention spans. They also freeze like a dream, which is perfect for any last minute guests that pop in for coffee.

This recipe also works just as well with nut-free alternatives like pea butter or soy butter.

MAKES 20–24 small cookies
PREP TIME 5 minutes
COOK TIME 6–8 minutes

1 cup (250 mL) unsalted nut butter

¾ cup (185 mL) cane sugar

1 egg, whisked

Good pinch of salt

¼ cup (60 mL) raw cacao nibs or mini chocolate chips (optional)

1. Preheat oven to 350°F (175°C) and line a baking sheet.
2. In a medium-sized bowl, mix the nut butter, sugar and egg together to form a thick dough. Stir in chocolate chips or cacao nibs, if using.
3. Portion out the dough in heaping teaspoon mounds onto the lined baking sheet. Roll quickly into balls then flatten slightly with the back of a fork.
4. Bake 6–8 minutes until lightly golden brown. They may look underbaked but will firm up once cooled. Freezer friendly.

SAVED MY LIFE: NUT-FREE BUTTERS FOR SCHOOL LUNCHES AND AFTER SCHOOL ACTIVITIES

I like to keep a jar of pea or soy butter on hand. They typically contain more sugar than I would like, but they are a lifesaver when you're in a pinch for a quick sandwich to send to school.

NUT BUTTER COOKIE TIP

- Depending on the brand of nut butter you use, some are looser than others, especially if you keep yours in the fridge. Nut butters stir in easily when at room temperature. Heat the nut butter–sugar mix in a small pot over low heat to loosen slightly, if needed.

(V, GF, NF, LS)

CREAMSICLE COCONUT TRUFFLES

For all my vegan friends out there, here is an easy low-sugar (and therefore convincingly guilt-free) sweet treat. Definitely a better choice than the Bounty bar I bought last time I was waiting in line at the drug store. The combination of orange zest and vanilla will give you that creamsicle flavour with just a hint of sweetness from the honey.

MAKES 12 truffles
PREP TIME 20 minutes
COOLING TIME 1 hour

2 Tbsp (30 mL) coconut oil

2 Tbsp (30 mL) honey or maple syrup

1 tsp (5 mL) Pure Vanilla Extract (see p. 14)

1 cup (250 mL) unsweetened shredded coconut

½ cup (125 mL) almond flour

1 tsp (5 mL) freshly grated orange zest

Pinch of salt

1. In a small saucepot, melt coconut oil with honey or maple syrup. Once melted, remove from heat and stir in vanilla.
2. In a medium-sized bowl, combine the coconut, almond flour, orange zest and salt. Pour the melted coconut and honey in and stir to combine.
3. Place in the fridge to firm up, about 15 minutes. Roll into truffle-sized balls. Place back in the fridge to set completely, about 1 hour. These truffles freeze very well.

SAVED MY LIFE: COCONUT OIL IS NOT JUST FOR COOKING

Coconut oil has removed many a morning's raccoon eyes from last night's black mascara.

Also, in a pinch, I have used it as a moisturizer, lip balm or hair treatment. It is truly multipurpose.

COCONUT OIL TIPS

- Coconut oil can be stored at room temperature for 2 years. That's pretty impressive.
- When buying coconut oil for its nutritional content, look for raw, cold-pressed virgin coconut oil. It is less processed.
- If you are looking for coconut oil with minimal coconut flavour, buy expeller-pressed oil. This type also has a higher smoke point.

(V, GF, LS)

SUPERNATURAL VEGAN BROWNIES

Describing a brownie as being raw and vegan may seem tasteless on my part, but you're going to have to trust me. These brownies are decadent and unbelievably delicious. The naturally sweet Medjool dates replace sugar. There are no eggs or butter involved, no baking, and this recipe is also gluten-free. You will just have to try them for yourself.

MAKES 36 brownies
SOAK TIME overnight
PREP TIME 25 minutes
SET TIME 2–3 hours
SPECIAL EQUIPMENT NEEDED food processor

1 cup (250 mL) raw walnuts

1⅔ oz (50 g) dark chocolate (60–70%), chopped

2 cups (500 mL) packed pitted Medjool dates (about 24)

½ cup (125 mL) raw cocoa powder

¼ cup (60 mL) nut or seed butter

2 tsp (10 mL) Pure Vanilla Extract (see p. 14)

½ cup (125 mL) unsweetened shredded coconut (optional)

Good pinch of salt

VEGAN CHOCOLATE GANACHE FROSTING

½ cup (125 mL) vegan milk of choice

8 oz (225 g) dark chocolate, finely chopped

Pinch of salt

1. Soak walnuts overnight in enough water to cover. Rinse, drain and set aside on a clean tea towel to soak up any residual moisture.
2. Line an 8 x 8-inch (20 x 20 cm) square pan with 2 strips of parchment paper, crisscrossed so it covers all 4 sides of the pan. Use binder clips to hold parchment to the sides of the pan (see Cool Fact p. 146)
3. Melt chopped chocolate in a double boiler over low heat and set aside.
4. Using a food processor, pulse and finely grind nuts.
5. Add dates and pulse a few times until broken up.
6. Add in remaining ingredients and melted chocolate and process to form a paste. This will eventually form into a ball in the processor.
7. Transfer to the lined pan and press to create an even layer with the back of a spoon. Cover and store in the fridge until frosting is ready.
8. Heat milk in a small saucepot over medium until steaming.
9. Place chopped chocolate in a medium-sized bowl. Pour over hot milk, sprinkle in salt and let sit for 3 minutes. The heat from the milk will be enough to melt the chocolate.
10. Whisk melted chocolate with milk until smooth. Pour frosting over the brownies and level out. Place back in the fridge to set, about 2 hours. Cut into small squares and serve.
11. Brownies are best stored in the fridge and freeze well.

BAKE SALE RECIPES TO GET YOU THROUGH THE YEAR

At the beginning of every school year I tell myself that I am going to make more of an effort to become involved at my kids' school. Then, just like that, the school year is over. Well, at least I contributed to all the bake sales!

Kids always want to help out when you are baking sweets for all their friends. With more and more food allergies popping up, it's nice to have access to gluten-free, nut-free and even egg-free options. Making a list of ingredients to go alongside your bake sale donations is always greatly appreciated.

(NF)

ONE GOOD CAKE (OR CUPCAKE) WITH DE-LIGHTFUL VANILLA ICING

You only need one really great cake and cupcake recipe, and this is mine.

I was looking for the easiest way to make a pink cake for a girly birthday without having to use food colouring. There is already so much artificial colouring being added to food and, as a parent, I am sure you have heard how some of these artificial food dyes may cause reactions and that they are something we quite possibly shouldn't be feeding our kids. So why not tint a really great vanilla cake recipe with a colourful fruit purée?

Puréed raspberries or blueberries mixed into this simple cake batter not only make it pink or blue, but also add moisture and subtle berry flavours. Perfect for kids' birthday parties, Valentine's Day, school functions and yes, bake sales.

MAKES two 8- or 9-inch (20 or 23 cm) round cakes or 24 cupcakes
PREP TIME 20 minutes
COOK TIME 20–25 minutes
SPECIAL EQUIPMENT NEEDED two 8- or 9-inch (20 or 23 cm) round cake pans, stand mixer with a paddle attachment or handheld mixer, hand-immersion blender or regular blender, fine mesh sieve or cheesecloth

- 1 cup (250 mL) unsalted butter, softened
- 1½ cups (375 mL) sugar
- 2½ cups (625 mL) cake and pastry flour
- ½ Tbsp (7 mL) baking powder
- ½ tsp (2 mL) baking soda
- Pinch of salt
- 4 eggs, at room temperature
- 1 tsp (5 mL) Pure Vanilla Extract (see p. 14)
- 2 cups (500 mL) fresh or thawed raspberries (for pink cake)
- 1 cup (250 mL) fresh or thawed blueberries (for blue cake)
- ½ cup (125 mL) milk or unsweetened milk alternative
- De-Lightful Vanilla Icing (recipe follows)

1. Preheat oven to 350°F (175°C). Grease and lightly flour two 8- or 9-inch (20 or 23 cm) pans and line each with a cut round of parchment (or line muffins tins).
2. Using a stand mixer with the paddle attachment or a handheld mixer, cream butter with sugar in a large bowl until light and fluffy, about 3–5 minutes depending on the temperature of the butter.
3. Meanwhile, in another bowl, whisk together the flour, baking powder, baking soda and salt.
4. Add eggs, one by one, into the butter-sugar mixture at medium speed, scraping down the sides in-between additions. Beat in vanilla.
5. Purée berries with milk in a blender, then pour through a fine mesh sieve or colander lined with cheesecloth to remove seeds and bits of skin. Measure 1 cup (250 mL) purée; if there is a little left over, drink it.
6. Add flour in 2 equal additions on low speed, alternating with your purée. Scape down the sides when needed and mix until everything is incorporated.
7. Divide batter into the 2 pans (or muffins tins, filling muffin liners half full). Bake cakes for 25 minutes (or cupcakes for 20 minutes), or until lightly browned on top and a toothpick comes out clean.
8. Place on a cooling rack and ice when completely cooled. I highly recommend icing the cake using the De-Lightful Vanilla Icing recipe.

ONE GOOD CAKE (OR CUPCAKE) WITH DE-LIGHTFUL VANILLA ICING CONTINUED . . .

(BF, NF)

DE-LIGHTFUL VANILLA ICING

MAKES about 5 cups (1.25 L)
PREP TIME 10 minutes
SPECIAL EQUIPMENT NEEDED stand mixer with a whisk attachment

2 cups (500 mL) whipping cream (35%)

One 8-oz (225 g) pkg cream cheese, softened at room temp (takes an hour)

½ cup (125 mL) icing sugar (or to taste)

2 tsp (10 mL) Pure Vanilla Extract (see p. 14)

1. Using a stand mixer with the whisk attachment, whip cream until soft peaks form. Set aside.
2. In a separate bowl, whip cream cheese until soft and aerated, about 3–5 minutes.
3. Add cream cheese to whipped cream and continue to beat on high with the whisk attachment until stiff peaks form. Beat in the sugar and vanilla, adding more sugar to taste.
4. Pipes very well; keep refrigerated.

SAVED MY LIFE: NO CAKE AND PASTRY FLOUR?

No cake and pastry flour? No problem. This substitution works in a pinch: ⅔ cup + ¼ cup (220 mL) all-purpose flour and 2 Tbsp (30 mL) cornstarch equals 1 cup (250 mL) cake and pastry flour.

CAKE TIP

- Adding "in additions" helps incorporate all ingredients evenly. I am not going to get all scientific with you here, but it does make a difference. It helps to emulsify the mixture. It also helps with the mess. If you add a whole bowl of really wet or dry ingredients in all at once, it's guaranteed that as soon as you turn the mixer on stuff is going to fly everywhere.

NOT-SO-COOL FACT: YOU ARE PROBABLY MEASURING YOUR FLOUR WRONG

It is kind of impossible to measure flour properly out of those narrow bags it's sold in—I can't believe not one flour company has attempted to change their packaging to make measuring flour easier. You want to scoop it right out of the bag with your measuring utensil because this makes the most logical sense, but this is not how you measure flour. This causes the flour to pack in, which then causes you to over-measure the flour.

The best way to measure flour is to weigh it (¼ lb/120 grams of flour equals 1 cup/250 mL). However, we don't all have scales, so this is the next best method: spoon flour into a dry measure until mounded at the top, then level it off with the back of a knife. Don't shake or pack it into the cup. This is almost impossible to do in or over the narrow flour bag without getting it everywhere, so I store my flour in a large wide container and measure overtop.

(GF, NF)

USE-UP-THE-ZUCCHINI OATMEAL CHOCOLATE CHIP COOKIES

I fell in love with organic fruit and vegetable delivery when my kids were small, and if you've ever tried to go grocery shopping with a newborn and a toddler in tow you'll understand why. Those weekly boxes saved my sanity and our dinner plates! The only trick was trying to figure out how to use up all the zucchini that arrived week after week. Not that I didn't love those green summery squash, but eventually my family started to revolt and I had to get creative. Originally a solution to the zucchini problem, these cake-like cookies quickly became a family favourite. Gluten-free and flavourful, they are great for school lunches and bake sales, not to mention they make a phenomenal ice cream sandwich.

MAKES 21–24 cookies
PREP TIME 20 minutes
COOK TIME 12–14 minutes
SPECIAL EQUIPMENT NEEDED stand mixer with a paddle attachment or hand held mixer, food processor or blender that grinds grains

- 1 cup (250 mL) finely grated zucchini (about 1 zucchini)
- 1 tsp (5 mL) salt
- 1 cup (250 mL) butter, softened
- 1 cup (250 mL) cane sugar
- ½ cup (125 mL) lightly packed dark brown sugar
- 1 egg
- 1 tsp (5 mL) Pure Vanilla Extract (see p. 14)
- 1 cup (250 mL) gluten-free oats, ground
- 1½ cups (375 mL) gluten-free oats
- 1¼ cups (310 mL) Gluten-Free All-Purpose Flour (see p. 24)
- ½ tsp (2 mL) xanthan (if not already added to the gluten-free flour)
- 1 tsp (5 mL) baking soda
- 2 Tbsp (30 mL) My Ground Seed Mix (see p. 44; optional)
- 1½ cups (375 mL) gluten-free chocolate chips

1. Preheat oven to 375°F (190°C) and line a baking sheet.
2. Place zucchini in a colander fit over a bowl. Sprinkle with salt and let sit for 10 minutes, then give it a good squeeze. The salt helps the zucchini release moisture. You want to get all the moisture out of the zucchini before folding it into the batter, so the cookies are not soggy.
3. In the meantime, beat butter with the sugars until light and fluffy, about 3–5 minutes. Add in the egg and vanilla and beat again until combined.
4. In a large bowl, stir together all remaining dry ingredients except the chocolate chips.
5. Beat dry ingredients into the butter-sugar mixture in 2 additions. Once combined, fold in the zucchini and chocolate chips.
6. Portion batter into 2-Tbsp (30 mL) mounds, spaced 2 inches (5 cm) apart on the baking sheet. Bake for 12–14 minutes, or until edges are golden brown and middles look just set, in batches if necessary.
7. Let rest 5 minutes before transferring to a cooling rack. Store in an airtight container when cooled. These cookies are freezer friendly.

SAVED MY LIFE: LOCAL FOOD DELIVERY SERVICES

Check out CSA (Community Shared Agriculture) services, which are committed to community growth and local farmers in your neighbourhood. This is like owning your own small share in a local farm.

These days you can get everything delivered right to your front door.

COOKIE TIPS

- Beat butter with sugars well to incorporate air into the mix and to start dissolving sugar into the butter.
- Adding flour to dough in additions helps get it evenly dispersed. It will also help keep the flour from scattering all over the counter.
- You can always refrigerate or freeze cookie dough, for freshly baked cookies anytime. Form dough into a log, roll in plastic wrap and slice for easier portioning.
- Reuse zucchini juice in soup or smoothies.

COOL FACT: BUTTER NOT SOFTENED?

Cut into small cubes and work it with the mixer or paddle attachment until softened.

(NF)

MY COFFEE SHOP BERRY MUFFINS

Here is my healthier homemade version of the classic coffee shop muffin. I use a combination of spelt and all-purpose flour, since I like the slightly nutty flavour spelt lends to baked goods. I also love adding my My Ground Seed Mix (see p. 44) to boost fibre and nutrients. If you have one of those children that pick out the berries, try this. My daughter has told me many times that the berries I use in my muffins are just way too big. If they use real berries in prepackaged baked goods, it is usually just specks of them, but frozen raspberries are super easy to crumble into smaller pieces if you prefer it that way.

MAKES 24 muffins
PREP TIME 20 minutes
BAKE TIME 15–20 minutes

2 cups (500 mL) spelt flour

2 cups (500 mL) all-purpose flour

¼ cup (60 mL) My Ground Seed Mix (see p. 44; optional)

4 tsp (20 mL) baking powder

Pinch of salt

1 cup (250 mL) cane sugar

2 eggs

1 cup (250 mL) milk of choice

1 cup (250 mL) buttermilk or plain yogurt

1 lemon, zested

1 tsp (5 mL) Pure Vanilla Extract (see p. 14)

⅔ cup (160 mL) butter or coconut oil, melted and cooled

2 cups (500 mL) raspberries or mixed berries, fresh or frozen

Multipurpose Crumble Topping (see p. 184; optional)

1. Preheat oven to 375°F (190°C). Line or grease muffin trays.
2. Whisk together the flours, seed mix, baking powder and salt in a large bowl.
3. In a separate large bowl, whisk sugar with the eggs, milk, buttermilk or yogurt, lemon zest and vanilla.
4. Pour the wet ingredients into the dry and stir to combine.
5. Fold in melted butter or coconut oil.
6. Fold in berries and portion into muffin trays, filling three-quarters full. Sprinkle over crumble topping if you wish.
7. Bake for 20 minutes or until a cake tester comes out clean. Let cool 5 minutes then transfer to a cooling rack.

SAVED MY LIFE: WHO NEEDS A CAKE TESTER?

A wooden or metal barbecue skewer, toothpick or knife works just fine.

MUFFIN TIPS

- Want a buttermilk peach version of this recipe? Substitute buttermilk for the milk and 2 cups (500 mL) diced peaches for the berries.
- Don't have a cooling rack? Lift muffins and place sideways in their trays, letting air circulate around their sides.

(GF, NF)

OH MY GLUTEN-FREE BROWNIES AND FAST FUDGY FROSTING

I adapted these super decadent brownies from a gluten-free baking episode I did on Best Recipes Ever. The method is super easy, so kids can make these themselves. When testing these brownies for the book, I timed my daughter making them instead of me, to prove to her that it isn't necessarily faster or easier making brownies from a box. I cut down on the amount of sugar from the original recipe and offer you some easy recipe substitutions.

The Fast Fudgy Frosting is my version of a recipe pieced together from what I can remember my mom making when I was a child. Her fast fudge frosting would go with almost any cake, square, cupcake, brownie or cookie. Plus you probably already have all the ingredients on hand, so it's great in a pinch. The flavour reminds me of being a kid again.

Once iced, I cut these brownies into small bite-sized squares for little one hitters, great for after a dinner party or an afternoon pick me up.

MAKES 16–25 brownies
PREP TIME 15 minutes
COOK TIME 30 minutes
SPECIAL EQUIPMENT NEEDED square pan (preferably 9 × 9 inch/23 × 23 cm)

1 cup (250 mL) butter

1¼ cups (310 mL) gluten-free semi-sweet or dark chocolate chips (or 10 oz/300 g chopped chocolate)

¼ cup (60 mL) milk, cream, buttermilk or any other unsweetened milk alternative

¼ cup (60 mL) white or brown rice flour

½ tsp (2 mL) gluten-free baking powder

½ tsp (2 mL) ground cinnamon

Pinch of salt

½–¾ cup (125–185 mL) light brown sugar (use ¾ cup/185 mL if using dark chocolate)

¼ cup (60 mL) raw cocoa powder, sifted

4 eggs

1 tsp (5 mL) Pure Vanilla Extract (see p. 14)

Fast Fudgy Frosting (recipe follows; optional) or Vegan Chocolate Ganache (see p. 153; optional)

1. Preheat oven to 350°F (175°C). Line a pan with 2 cut strips of parchment, crisscrossing so that the bottom and all 4 sides are evenly covered.
2. Melt butter with chocolate and milk in a heavy-bottomed saucepot over medium heat until the chocolate has just melted, stirring occasionally. Do not let this mixture simmer or boil, since chocolate is prone to burning. Set aside.
3. While the chocolate is melting, in a large bowl whisk together rice flour, baking powder, cinnamon, salt and the brown sugar. Sift in cocoa powder then whisk in eggs and vanilla until combined.
4. While whisking, slowly pour the melted chocolate into the egg mixture (do not pour all at once in order to avoid scrambling the eggs). I find kids need an extra pair of hands to help with this step—one set to hold the bowl and whisk, while the other pours in the melted chocolate.
5. Pour into the parchment-lined pan and bake for 30 minutes or until a toothpick comes out clean.
6. Let cool, frost if desired and refrigerate. Best kept cold. Freezer friendly.

(GF, NF)

FAST FUDGY FROSTING

MAKES 1 cup (250 mL)
COOK TIME 5 minutes
SPECIAL EQUIPMENT NEEDED stand mixer with a paddle attachment (or hand mixer)

¼ cup (60 mL) butter

¼ cup (60 mL) unsweetened milk of choice

3 Tbsp (45 mL) raw cocoa powder

Pinch of salt

1 cup (250 mL) icing sugar

1 tsp (5 mL) Pure Vanilla Extract (see p. 14)

1. In a small saucepot over medium heat, melt butter with the milk, cocoa powder and salt until the butter is just melted and the cocoa powder is fully absorbed into the mixture.
2. Transfer to a bowl and beat in icing sugar.
3. Pour on top of brownies or cake while icing is still slightly warm, making it easier to pour and spread. Use the back of a spoon, an offset spatula or a knife to spread.

SAVED MY LIFE: HOW TO CUT THE PERFECT SLICE

Place a knife in a glass of very hot water; the heat from the knife will glide through any cake or cookie with one clean swipe. With each section you cut, wipe the knife with a paper towel and dip back into the hot water.

FROSTING TIP

- For frosting cupcakes, let the icing cool down, since it will thicken as it cools and is easier to spread.

BROWNIE TIPS

- I keep this recipe nut-free so the kids can bring them to school; however, these brownies are even more heavenly when you add 1 cup (125 mL) chopped walnuts or pecans.
- Gluten-free chocolate can be more challenging to find, but any good health food store or section of your local grocer should carry it. Most quality chocolate is naturally gluten-free but it is not always labelled as such, or may have been processed in a facility that is not gluten-free. Cocoa Camino is one of my go-to brands.

(GF, NF)

POPCORN BALLS

Recipes that involve arts and crafts are my all-time favourites. Not only do I get to cook, but I can also get out the big box of art supplies and get kids to decorate, which occupies them for at least a half an hour. I have made these for loot bags at birthday parties, as Halloween treats for neighbours and at adult parties (and, of course, at bake sales).

MAKES 12 popcorn balls
PREP TIME 5 minutes
BAKE TIME 15 minutes
SPECIAL EQUIPMENT NEEDED plastic wrap or cellophane bags, coloured ribbon, name tags or anything else kids want to decorate bags with

10 cups (2.5 L) popped popcorn (about ½ cup/125 mL kernels)

2 cups (500 mL) graham crackers (about 15 crackers), broken into ½-inch (1 cm) pieces

One ½-lb (250 g) bag mini marshmallows, divided

¼ cup (60 mL) butter

1 tsp (5 mL) Pure Vanilla Extract (see p. 14)

2 oz (60 g) bittersweet chocolate and/or 2 oz (60 g) white chocolate, finely chopped for drizzling (optional)

Neutral-flavoured oil or butter, for greasing

1. In a large greased roasting pan, toss together the popcorn, graham crackers and 1 cup (250 mL) of the marshmallows. Set aside.
2. In a large saucepan, melt the remaining marshmallows with butter over medium-low heat, stirring constantly until smooth. Remove from heat. Stir in vanilla. Immediately pour over the popcorn mixture; stir with a greased spatula to coat. Let cool enough to handle.
3. With greased hands, roll popcorn into balls, each ball containing about ¾ cup (185 mL), and place on a lined tray; let cool. If your hands start getting sticky, just wash them and grease again.
4. In a heatproof bowl over a saucepan of hot (not boiling) water, melt bittersweet or white chocolate, if using. Dip a fork in the melted chocolate to help drizzle half of it over the popcorn balls. Refrigerate balls until chocolate is set, about 10 minutes. Turn balls over and drizzle with the remaining chocolate; refrigerate until set. Hey, if you have the time, melt both types of chocolate separately and drizzle both.
5. Once popcorn is set, you can package separately in food-safe bags, tie with ribbons and add name tags. For fun you can get out the arts and crafts box to let kids decorate the bags. This should occupy them for at least 30 minutes.

SAVED MY LIFE: GREASING UTENSILS WHEN DEALING WITH STICKY STUFF

Buttering or greasing hands, cooking utensils, even measuring cups will help immensely when dealing with sticky stuff in the kitchen. Even when measuring honey I will grease the measuring cup so that the honey comes out easily.

POPCORN BALL TIPS

- Wrap individually in plastic wrap or small clear food-safe gift bags and store for up to 24 hours. Decorate bags and get creative.
- You can omit the graham crackers and add 1 cup (250 mL) candy-coated chocolates for something more colourful (and a little sweeter).
- ¼ cup (60 mL) of popcorn kernels typically makes 5–6 cups (1.25–1.5 L) popcorn. However, not all kernels will pop, and popcorn varies in size. It is always better to just make more than you think you may need, since leftovers will always get eaten.

(V, NF)

NO-BAKE CHOCOLATE CLUTTER COOKIES

Every few months I declutter my pantry and look for ways to use up any dried goods I have lying around. Bulk cereal my kids begged for but never finished, half-filled bags of unused baking chocolate, seeds, dried fruit, flaked coconut and partially filled bags of oats just lying around, not getting eaten, drives me a little nuts. This easy recipe that kids can customize and make themselves is the perfect way to make use of all your pantry clutter. They taste great with nuts but I use seeds instead for safe school treats.

MAKES 14–16 cookies
TOTAL TIME 15 minutes

6 oz (175 g) semi-sweet, dark or white chocolate

2 Tbsp (30 mL) coconut oil

1 tsp (5 mL) Pure Vanilla Extract (see p. 14)

Pinch of salt

2 cups (500 mL) corn flakes

1 cup (250 mL) puffed rice

¼ cup (60 mL) sunflower seeds

¼ cup (60 mL) pumpkin seeds

1. Line a baking sheet.
2. Melt chocolate with coconut oil in a double boiler or bowl set over a pot of barely simmering water, making sure the bottom of the bowl is not touching the water. Stir occasionally.
3. Once melted, remove from heat and stir in vanilla and salt.
4. In a large bowl, combine all remaining ingredients. Pour melted chocolate overtop and fold with a spatula to coat. Lay tablespoon-sized cookie clumps on the lined baking sheet.
5. Place in the fridge to cool until set.

SOMETHING FOR DESSERT?

This section was written with moderation in mind, but I have a formidable sweet tooth. And baking I do out of pure pleasure, not necessity.

It is always lovely to finish a meal with a bite of something sweet, but it shouldn't be expected. A bowl of fresh fruit with a dollop of whipped cream is a pretty standard weekly after-dinner affair in our house. A few squares of chocolate makes me pretty darn happy as well.

If you feel the itch to bake though, as I do, then here are some truly great recipes, from simple to spectacular. I hope you enjoy. I would also like to use a quote from Julia Child at this time: "Everything in moderation, even moderation."

(GF, NF)

VANILLA BEAN PUDDING (AKA PASTRY CREAM)

I distinctly remember those small tin cans of pudding in my school lunch. Pudding was something we always bought at a grocery store and never made from scratch.

Then I took my first pastry course and my mind was blown. I learned about pastry cream and realized that my favourite custard-filled French and Italian pastries were basically filled with pudding. Pudding, aka pastry cream, should not be bought on a grocery store shelf, especially since it is easily made at home with just a few simple ingredients.

Dairy-free milk alternatives are also easily substituted into this recipe. I cut back on the sugar amounts, since I prefer desserts subtly sweet. I love using this recipe in pies, tarts and cream puffs, between cake layers, tossed with berries or (my all-time favourite) soaking into layers of angel food cake in my Summer Berry Trifle (see p. 176).

MAKES 6 servings
PREP TIME 5 minutes
COOK TIME 15 minutes
SET TIME 1 hour
SPECIAL EQUIPMENT NEEDED fine mesh sieve

- 1 vanilla bean, split lengthwise and scraped of seeds
- 2 cups (500 mL) unsweetened milk of choice
- ½ cup (125 mL) sugar
- 3 Tbsp (45 mL) cornstarch
- Pinch of salt
- 4 egg yolks
- 2 Tbsp (30 mL) butter

1. Scrape seeds from split vanilla bean using the back of a spoon or knife and add both the pod and seeds to a heavy-bottomed saucepot. Pour in milk and place over medium heat until steaming. Turn off heat, cover and let steep for 10 minutes, infusing the vanilla into the milk as you would tea.
2. Meanwhile, whisk sugar, cornstarch and salt together in a large bowl. Whisk in the egg yolks to make a thick pale-yellow paste.
3. After steeping, remove vanilla pod from hot milk (wash well and set aside for another use, see p. 14). Very slowly ladle the hot milk into the egg mixture, whisking constantly. If you find the bowl with the egg mixture is moving around too much, call out for an extra pair of hands or wrap a damp tea towel around the bottom of the bowl on the counter. This will keep it from moving.
4. Rinse out the saucepot but do not dry. (The slight wetness helps prevent scorching in the next step.) Return custard to the saucepot and place over medium heat. Stir with a heat-resistant spatula or wooden spoon until the mixture starts to thicken and barely reaches a boil, about 3–5 minutes. Don't worry if you get some lumps.
5. Remove from heat and immediately pour through a mesh strainer into a bowl. Whisk in butter until melted.
6. Once pudding has cooled slightly, cover with plastic wrap pressed against the surface, creating a seal and preventing a skin from forming. Refrigerate until set.

SAVED MY LIFE: THE EASIEST WAY TO CRACK EGGS

If you crack two eggs against one another, one will always break while the other stays intact. Long gone are the days of using the side of a bowl or the edge of a knife. Just crack one egg against another and continue doing it until all eggs are cracked. Genius right? The last egg you will have to crack elsewhere.

PUDDING TIPS

- For chocolate pudding, whisk in 2 oz (60 g) finely chopped or grated chocolate into the pudding instead of the butter.
- To make vanilla mousse, fold 1 cup (250 mL) whipped cream into the pudding after it has chilled. This produces an airy dessert or filling.
- For Earl Grey pudding, infuse 2 tsp (10 mL) loose-leaf Earl Grey tea or 1 bag into milk. Strain and continue with the recipe.
- Tempering is bringing an egg mixture up gradually in temperature to avoid curdling. See Cool Fact on page 85 for more information.

COOL FACT: HOW TO KEEP THINGS IN PLACE

Placing anti-slip mats or damp tea towels around the bottoms of bowls and under cutting boards is something I learned about in culinary school. When working in a restaurant kitchen, you don't want to have to ask for another pair of hands to hold a bowl down, or have a cutting board move around on you. Buy a cheap anti-slip mat, the same thing you buy to go under rugs or to line drawers with. It keeps your board secure and makes chopping much safer.

(GF, NF, LS)

FIVE-MINUTE, FIVE-INGREDIENT LEMON CURD

We all know that everything is better with butter, but everything is also lovelier with lemon! Thankfully there is plenty of both in my Five-Minute, Five-Ingredient Lemon Curd.

This recipe is slightly different than the traditional version you may know. The honey adds a complex sweetness and, because I add extra lemon zest at the end, it's even tangier. Bright, citrusy and velvety smooth, this curd is a go-to for last minute desserts. It's the perfect topping for almost everything: dollop it on fresh scones or pancakes, toss it in a bowl with some whipped cream and a handful of raspberries or use it as a filling with my Honey Angel Food Cake (see p. 174) or Summer Berry Trifle (see p. 176). If you're like my kids or me, you'll enjoy this lovely lemon delicacy on its own by the spoonful!

MAKES 1½ cups (375 mL)
PREP TIME 5 minutes
COOK TIME 5 minutes
SPECIAL EQUIPMENT NEEDED good heavy-bottomed saucepot, microplane (optional)

- 3 eggs
- ⅓ cup (80 mL) honey
- ½ cup (125 mL) fresh lemon juice, strained
- Pinch of salt
- 1 Tbsp (15 mL) lemon zest
- 6 Tbsp (90 mL) butter, cut into 6 cubes

1. In a medium-sized saucepot, whisk together the eggs, honey, lemon juice and salt. Place over medium heat and stir with a heatproof spatula, wooden spoon or whisk until the mixture starts steaming and thickens enough to coat the back of a spoon. Turn off the heat, whisk in lemon zest and butter cubes until melted, about a minute.
2. Transfer curd into a bowl and place a layer of plastic wrap on the surface of the curd as it cools. This will prevent a skin from forming.
3. Serve warm or cold. Curd will thicken as it chills. Curd lasts up to 1 week in the fridge.

LEMON TIPS

- This may be self explanatory, but it is best to zest the lemon first, then juice.
- Only zest the coloured rind of the citrus, never the white pith (which is very bitter).
- Room-temperature lemons juice more easily than cold ones. Also, give your citrus a good roll with your hands before juicing.

COOL FACT: YOU CAN FREEZE LEMON CURD

Did you know that you can freeze lemon curd? Just thaw and eat.

(GF, NF, LS)

HONEY SWEET ANGEL FOOD CAKE

There's a reason why this cake was named the food of the angels. Light as air and subtly sweet, it makes a perfect threesome with fresh fruit and whipped cream.

Angel food cake is my birthday cake of choice. It rekindles memories of my mom baking it when I was a little girl. Also, it is mostly egg whites, so how bad can it be for me? There has to be something good about having that much protein for dessert.

I made one significant change to the traditional recipe—I use honey instead of superfine sugar. With its more-intense flavour profile, I was able to cut the amount of sugar usually required in half.

This cake has only six ingredients and is very easy to make, you just have to remember two things: sift the flour three times, and fold gently.

Want an amazing dessert showstopper? Use this cake in my Summer Berry Trifle (see p. 176).

MAKES 8 servings
PREP TIME 25 minutes
BAKE TIME 35–40 minutes
COOK TIME 1 hour
SPECIAL EQUIPMENT NEEDED flour sifter or fine mesh sieve, tube cake pan, stand mixer with a whisk attachment or handheld mixer

- 1 cup (250 mL) cake and pastry flour
- ¼ tsp (1 mL) salt
- 12 egg whites
- 1 tsp (5 mL) cream of tartar
- ¾ cup (185 mL) cane sugar, honey or maple syrup
- 2 tsp (10 mL) Pure Vanilla Extract (see p. 14)

1. Preheat oven 350°F (175°C).
2. Sift flour with salt twice into a bowl.
3. In a large bowl, beat egg whites on medium-high with the whisk attachment until foamy, about 1 minute. Add cream of tartar and beat again on medium-high until soft peaks form, 2–3 minutes. While gradually drizzling in the honey, continue to beat until stiff peaks form, 3–4 minutes. Beat in vanilla.
4. Transfer to the widest bowl you have. Sift flour for the third time over the egg whites, in 2 additions, folding gently with a spatula after each addition until just combined. Don't overmix and deflate the airy goodness.
5. Gently spoon batter into an ungreased pan. Using a knife or barbecue skewer, cut through the batter to release any unwanted air bubbles.
6. Bake until golden and cake springs back when lightly pressed with fingers, 35–40 minutes.
7. Run a knife around the sides and bottom of the pan to help release the cake. Turn the pan upside-down onto a cooling rack for 1 hour, so the cake does not collapse onto itself.
8. Once cooled, wrap cake securely in plastic wrap and store at room temperature for up to 2 days, or up to a week in the fridge.

SAVED MY LIFE: STORING LEFTOVER EGG WHITES AND YOLKS

Whites can be frozen or stored in an airtight container in the fridge. Yolks, however, will get pasty if left like this. Place yolks in an airtight container, covered with a little water in the fridge. Pour off water before use.

ANGEL FOOD CAKE TIPS

- This cake is best cut by a serrated knife.
- Don't grease the pan. It is harder to climb up a ladder if it is wet or greasy, and we want this cake to climb.
- Use leftover yolks to make the Vanilla Bean Pudding (see p. 170).
- For a Chocolate Orange Angel Food Cake, replace ¼ cup (60 mL) flour with ¼ cup (60 mL) cocoa powder and substitute the vanilla with 1 Tbsp (15 mL) orange flower water.
- To make the cake gluten-free, use ¾ cup + 4 tsp (205 mL) Gluten-Free All-Purpose Flour (see p. 24) instead of the cake and pastry flour, then add 3 Tbsp (45 mL) cornstarch; this will create a lighter-weight gluten-free cake and pastry flour. Cake will not rise as high as with regular cake and pastry flour, but it tastes just as good.

(NF)

SUMMER BERRY TRIFLE

The double explosion of layered vanilla custard and lemon curd, embraced by honey-kissed angel food cake, makes this quite possibly the best dessert ever. It is also stunning to look at. Grownups adore the airy light "not too sweet" quality, while kids love the whipped cream and berries. It is one of those desserts where everyone has seconds.

A good trifle needs time to relax a bit. You want to let the flavours mingle. If you are looking for a show-stopping dessert and want to have it all done the day before, this is it. However, double check to make sure you have room to store it in the fridge.

MAKES 8–10 servings
PREP TIME 15 minutes
COOK TIME 1 hour
ASSEMBLY TIME 15 minutes
SPECIAL EQUIPMENT NEEDED large glass dessert bowl or trifle bowl or any clean clear vessel with relatively straight sides (flower vases work as well as old fishbowls)

2 cups (500 mL) whipped cream (35%)

¼ cup (60 mL) maple syrup

1 store-bought angel food cake or Honey Sweet Angel Food Cake (see p. 174), cut into 2-inch (5 cm) cubes, divided

1 recipe Vanilla Bean Pudding (see p. 170)

3–4 cups (750–1000 mL) strawberries, hulled and thinly sliced, divided

1 recipe Five-Minute, Five-Ingredient Lemon Curd (see p. 172)

OPTIONAL GARNISHES

A few whole strawberries

A few sprigs of mint

Handful of slivered almonds

Crumbled amaretti cookies

1. Whip cream with maple syrup to stiff peaks. Set aside.
2. Layer trifle starting with a third of the cubed angel food cake on the bottom. Spread cake with half of the vanilla pudding, a third of the cut strawberries and a third of the whipped cream. For the second layer, use another third of the cubed cake, then spread out a layer of the lemon curd, a third of the cut strawberries and a third of the whipped cream. For the last layer, finish off with the remaining cake, pudding, strawberries and whipped cream on top.
3. Store in the fridge up to 1 day ahead. Garnish just before serving with whole or sliced strawberries, torn mint leaves, slivered almonds or crumbled amaretti cookies.

SAVED MY LIFE: SMALL OFFSET SPATULA

There is something about the size of these little spatulas that makes them perfect for just about everything. From icing cupcakes to flipping mini pancakes, I am always reaching for my small offset spatula. It also fits in my back pocket nicely.

TRIFLE TIPS

- You can make any kind of cake into a trifle and it doesn't always have to be a huge masterpiece. Mini trifles are super cute for small intimate gatherings.
- Christmas trifle? Try my Chocolate Orange Angel Food Cake variation (see p. 175), and use winter fruit like pomegranates, poached pears, marinated cherries or mandarin segments for inspiration. Any fruit, fruit compote, fruity sauce or jam works.
- Booze this trifle up. No harm drizzling in a little kirsch, limoncello or cognac, especially around the holidays. It's also a great idea if the cake you are using is a little on the dry side.

(NF)

CHOCOLATE FOOL LOAF

The sheer amount of chocolate in this cake-like loaf guarantees it's going to be great. The secret is the veiled, finely grated zucchini. It melts into the batter as it bakes, making the cake super dense and moist, almost like eating bread pudding.

I actually prefer eating this cake after it has been refrigerated, served cold in cubes with a warm fruit compote like my Berry Vanilla Rhubarb Compote (see p. 43) and freshly whipped cream.

MAKES 2 loaves
PREP TIME 20 minutes
BAKE TIME 1 hour
SPECIAL EQUIPMENT NEEDED grater or food processor, stand mixer with a paddle attachment (optional)

2 large or 3 regular-sized zucchini, finely grated

3 cups (750 mL) cake and pastry flour

½ Tbsp (7 mL) baking powder

½ Tbsp (7 mL) baking soda

Pinch of salt

2 tsp (10 mL) ground cinnamon

½ tsp (2 mL) freshly grated nutmeg

½ tsp (2 mL) ground ginger

1 cup (250 mL) coconut oil, melted

2 cups (500 mL) sugar

1 egg

¼ cup (60 mL) ground flax

2 tsp (10 mL) Pure Vanilla Extract (see p. 14)

2 cups (500 mL) grated semi-sweet or dark chocolate (about 10 oz/300 g)

1. Preheat oven to 325°F (160°C) and grease 2 pans with coconut oil.
2. Place zucchini in a colander over a bowl to drain. Collect and reserve zucchini liquid after about 10 minutes.
3. In a large bowl, sift flour with the baking powder, soda, salt and spices.
4. In a second large bowl, beat together the melted coconut oil, sugar, egg, ground flax, vanilla and ½ cup (125 mL) of the reserved zucchini liquid. This can be done by hand with a whisk, but it's easier in a stand mixer fit with a paddle attachment.
5. Stir in sifted ingredients in 2 additions until just combined. Fold in grated zucchini and chocolate.
6. Pour into the prepared pans and bake for 1 hour or until a cake tester, toothpick or barbecue skewer inserted into the centre comes out clean.
7. Cool in pans for 10 minutes and remove.
8. Serve warm or cold. Freezer friendly.

SAVED MY LIFE: GRATING OR CHOPPING CHOCOLATE WITH A FOOD PROCESSOR

If you have to grate a lot of chocolate, I highly recommend using your food processor. It will save lots of time, and your hands.

(GF, NF, LS)

GINGER, PEACH AND WILD BLUEBERRY CRISP

People will eat dessert if they feel it is good for them, and what is a great meal without a great dessert? Crisps are my favourite way to celebrate local seasonal fruit, and I packed as much healthy goodness as I could into this recipe. The combination of fresh ginger, orange and vanilla bean are a little unexpected but really spice things up. I have added a fibre blast with my Ground Seed Mix combined into the topping, plus reduced the sugar.

My favourite part of making any crisp is that leftovers double as an ideal breakfast companion to yogurt. I may actually like crisps better the next day, cold, spooned right out of the casserole dish.

MAKES 8 servings
PREP TIME 20 minutes
COOK TIME 30 minutes
SPECIAL EQUIPMENT NEEDED pie plate, small casserole dish or square pan, baking sheet, grater, microplane

½ cup (125 mL) brown sugar, honey or maple syrup (or a combination)

3 Tbsp (45 mL) cornstarch

2 tsp (10 mL) freshly grated ginger

1 Tbsp (15 mL) orange zest

3 Tbsp (45 mL) orange juice (about ½ orange)

1 tsp (5 mL) Pure Vanilla Extract (see p. 14) or seeds scraped from ½ vanilla pod

7–8 cups (1.75–2 L) peach wedges (about 3 lb/1.4 kg peaches)

1 cup (250 mL) wild blueberries

CRISP TOPPING

1 cup (250 mL) oats

⅓ cup (80 mL) My Ground Seed Mix (see p. 44)

⅓ cup (80 mL) spelt flour, all-purpose flour or Gluten-Free All-Purpose Flour (see p. 24)

½ cup (125 mL) packed dark brown sugar

½ tsp (2 mL) ground ginger

¼ tsp (1 mL) ground nutmeg

2 tsp (10 mL) orange zest

Pinch of salt

½ cup (125 mL) cold butter, grated

½ cup (125 mL) coarsely chopped pecans (optional)

1. Preheat oven to 375°F (190°C). Grease a pie plate, casserole dish or square pan with butter.
2. In a large bowl, whisk together the sugar, cornstarch, grated ginger, orange zest, juice and vanilla.
3. Add peaches and blueberries, stir to coat and pour into a pie plate or casserole dish. Set aside.
4. Make crisp topping by mixing oats with the ground seeds, flour, sugar, spices, orange zest and salt. Grate in the cold butter and mix with hands until crumbly. If not baking immediately, place topping in the fridge to keep cold, otherwise sprinkle crisp topping overtop the fruit.
5. Place the crisp on a baking sheet to catch any overflowing bubbling molten fruit. Bake in a preheated oven for 25 minutes. Remove, sprinkle pecans overtop and bake again for an additional 5–10 minutes or until fruit is bubbling and topping is golden. If topping seems to be getting too brown before fruit is bubbling, loosely tent with foil.
6. Rest on a cooling rack for at least 20 minutes before serving. Serve warm or cold.

FRUIT CRISP TIPS

- Individual-serving fruit crisps are super cute. Bake time decreases depending on the size of ramekins, but you can tell they are done when the fruit is bubbling and the topping is browned.
- Alternate fruit combos? Pick a fruit that holds its shape when baked or combine different types of fruits; apples, pears, plums and peaches are all great in crisps, especially when combined with seasonal berries.

COOL FACT: WILD BLUEBERRIES ARE WAY BETTER

Smaller, deeper in colour and tastier, wild blueberries have double the amount of antioxidants compared to cultivated (farmed) ones. Buy "wild" blueberries, frozen fresh, in most major grocers to enjoy their benefits year round.

(NF)

ALL-THE-CHOCOLATE CHOCOLATE CHIP COOKIES

Baking cookies is a common occurrence at my house, and while that means my house typically smells of freshly baked cookies, it also typically means a few kids are destroying the kitchen. I decided that if my kids really want cookies, they were going to have to learn to bake them themselves.

We have a few great cookie recipes that the kids and I rotate through, so I felt the need to include more than just one cookie recipe. I also felt the need for it to be over the top, because every now and then you need something sinful.

There is a lot of chocolate in these cookies. They contain no cocoa powder, just a whole lot of pure melted chocolate—plus chocolate chunks, so you can just imagine. Or, instead of imagining, get in the kitchen and make them yourself.

MAKES 12 large or 22 small cookies
PREP TIME 15 minutes
COOK TIME 8–10 minutes

8 oz (225 g) bittersweet chocolate, chopped

3 Tbsp (45 mL) butter

1 Tbsp (15 mL) ground espresso (optional)

¼ cup (60 mL) packed dark brown sugar

2 eggs

1 tsp (5 mL) Pure Vanilla Extract (see p. 14)

½ cup (125 mL) all-purpose flour

¼ tsp (1 mL) baking powder

Pinch of salt

¾ cup (185 mL) semi-sweet chocolate chips or chunks (about 3 oz/90 g)

½ cup (125 mL) raw pumpkin seeds

½ cup (125 mL) pistachios (optional)

1. Preheat oven to 350°F (175°C). Line 2 baking sheets, or if you only have 1 then bake in batches.
2. Melt chopped bittersweet chocolate with the butter (and espresso, if using) in a small saucepot over low heat.
3. In a large bowl, whisk together the brown sugar, eggs and vanilla.
4. In a small bowl, whisk together the flour, baking powder and salt.
5. Once the chocolate is melted, let cool slightly if needed and whisk into the egg and sugar mixture. You don't want the hot chocolate to scramble the eggs.
6. Pour in the flour mixture and stir until well incorporated. Stir in chocolate chunks, pumpkin seeds and pistachios, if using.
7. Drop in mounds: for larger cookies use about ¼ cup (60 mL) each, or for smaller cookies use about 1 Tbsp (15 mL). Place on a baking sheet 2 inches (5 cm) apart.
8. Bake 10 minutes for larger, 7–8 minutes for smaller cookies, or until tops have cracks and cookies have a dull sheen. Cool on a wire rack.

STAUB

(NF)

PIE! AND THE PERFECT FLAKY PASTRY DOUGH

Northing compares to a good piece of pie . . . so here is one really great pie recipe that you can fill with your choice of seasonal fruit. You have with the option of making it with a double crust or the Multipurpose Crumble Topping (see p. 184). You choose.

Serve warm, topped with melty ice cream or—my all-time favourite—in cold forkfuls right out of the fridge.

MAKES 8 servings
PREP TIME 30 minutes
COOK TIME 40–45 minutes
SPECIAL EQUIPMENT NEEDED 9-inch (23 cm) pie plate, rolling pin

1 single crust or double crust Perfect Flaky Pastry Dough (recipe follows)

6 cups (1.5 L) pitted, sliced or cubed fruit (about 2 lb/900 g)

½–¾ cup (125–185 mL) brown or white sugar (depending on how sweet you like it)

2 Tbsp (30 mL) cornstarch

½ a lemon, juiced

1 Tbsp (15 mL) Pure Vanilla Extract (see p. 14) or 1 vanilla bean, seeds scraped

Pinch of salt

1 Tbsp (15 mL) orange or lemon zest (optional)

1 tsp (5 mL) ground cinnamon (optional)

¼ tsp (1 mL) ground nutmeg (optional)

2 tsp (10 mL) grated fresh ginger (optional)

¼ tsp (1 mL) ground allspice (optional)

Multipurpose Crumble Topping (see p. 184; optional)

1 Tbsp (15 mL) butter

1 egg, beaten, for egg wash (double crust only)

1. Preheat oven to 400°F (200°C).
2. Roll out pie dough into a 12-inch (30 cm) circle, according to the Perfect Flaky Pastry Dough method. Refrigerate dough in a pie plate while preparing the fruit filling.
3. Place all prepared fruit in a large bowl. Toss with sugar, cornstarch, lemon juice, vanilla, salt and any optional ingredients listed. Let sit for 15 minutes.
4. If making a double crust pie, roll out the second disc at this time, or make the crumble topping.
5. Fit pie crust in the plate with the fruit and any juices. Dot with butter.
6. Cover with the second crust, trimming any overhang more than ½ inch (1 cm) beyond the lip. Tuck double overhang underneath itself and flute your edges, or just use a fork to crimp. Make sure you provide at least 1 vent by making a few slits with a knife. Brush with egg wash. If using a crumble topping, sprinkle topping overtop fruit.
7. Place pie on a baking sheet to prevent any bubbling fruit from dripping. Bake 20 minutes, then reduce heat to 350°F (175°C) and continue to bake an additional 20 minutes, or until juices are bubbling and crust is golden. Transfer to a wire rack for at least 1 hour to cool before serving.

PIE TIPS

- Dotting the fruit with butter adds an extra layer of richness to your pie.
- Pie is better after it has cooled. I like to bake my pies first thing in the morning to let everything firm up a bit, but if not, nobody ever seems to mind a runny pie.

PIE! AND THE PERFECT FLAKY PASTRY DOUGH CONTINUED . . .

(NF, LS)

PERFECT FLAKY PASTRY DOUGH

MAKES 2 single pie crusts or 1 double
PREP TIME 10 minutes
COOK TIME 2–24 hours
SPECIAL EQUIPMENT NEEDED rolling pin, box grater, clean pillow case (optional)

2½ cups (625 mL) all-purpose flour

1 tsp (5 mL) salt

1 lemon, lime or orange, zested (optional for flavoured crust)

1 tsp (5 mL) ground cinnamon (optional for flavoured crust)

3 Tbsp (45 mL) sugar (for sweet pastry crust)

⅔ cup (160 mL) very cold or frozen butter

⅓ cup (80 mL) frozen lard

6 Tbsp (90 mL) ice-cold water

1 Tbsp (15 mL) Pure Vanilla Extract (see p. 14)

1. In a large bowl, whisk flour with the salt and any optional flavourings.
2. The easiest way to make pastry is to coarsely grate the cold fat into the flour. Simple—no food processor, stand mixer, pastry blender or knives. Use your box grater to coarsely grate butter and lard. Add to flour mix and fold in with fingers, coating grated fat with flour.
3. Measure out the ice-cold water and mix in vanilla.
4. Add 5 Tbsp (75 mL) water-vanilla mixture to the pastry and mix with hands until the dough starts to come together, adding more cold liquid if needed.
5. Transfer dough to a clean surface and give it a good quick knead until the dough comes together enough to form 2 round discs. Wrap each disc in 2 layers of plastic wrap. Store in the fridge and let rest at least 2 hours, preferably overnight, before rolling.
6. Lightly dust surface (or a pillow case—see Saved My Life below) and a rolling pin with flour. Have a pie plate nearby and roll out the pastry to fit the pie plate. Any overhang can be trimmed or tucked under after. Roll away from you and from the centre out. Rotate your pastry as you roll and flip over a few times to make sure the bottom doesn't stick, dusting with more flour if necessary. If you totally screw up, gather and press pastry together to form a ball, wrap in plastic wrap and let rest again in the fridge for at least 30 minutes before rolling.
7. Transfer pastry to pie plate by gently rolling the dough around the rolling pin, lifting and rolling it out overtop of the pie plate. Trim with kitchen shears or tuck overhang under and crimp.

SAVED MY LIFE: CLEAN COTTON PILLOWCASE

This simple trick, passed on to me from pastry chef Laura White, makes rolling out pie dough easy. Dust a clean pillowcase with flour and use this to roll your pastry on. The flour gets into the weave of the fabric, avoiding an over-floured surface and preventing you from handling the pastry too much. All you have to do is rotate the pillowcase instead of the actual dough when you roll. Genius! I have a pillowcase tucked away in my kitchen drawer just for this purpose.

PASTRY CRUST TIPS

- Pastry loves to rest in the cold. In the fridge, the flour absorbs moisture, the fat gets a chance firm up again and the glutens relax, making it easier to roll. Thirty minutes is the absolute minimum resting time, but you may still encounter shrinkage when baked. The longer it rests the better. If time permits, I prefer to make my pastry the day before I need it.
- It's ok if your dough is more on the moist side than the dry. You have to roll it out on a floured surface anyway, and it's harder to roll out dry crumbly dough than moist.
- Don't be afraid to give the dough a light knead or press it together. Everyone warns against overkneading; yes, we don't want the heat of our hands to melt all the fat, but we still need the dough to come together enough to roll out later. This is where a little practice comes into play. You want those streaks or pieces of fat marbled throughout the dough, and you want the dough to be able to be pressed together and form a ball. Don't worry if there are a few crumbs or dry bits.
- Adding the vanilla extract not only creates more flavour, but the alcohol helps as well. Gluten cannot form when mixed with alcohol, so this acts as a gluten inhibitor.
- Butter or lard? I am fortunate to have a supplier of grass-fed lard. I order it in blocks, freeze it and, when needed, just grate it off the block. To me, a perfect pie crust is one that uses a combination of both. Butter gives it decadent flavour, while the lard provides more flake. If you can't find a butcher that will sell you rendered lard, use butter (don't use the shelf stable vegetable shortening).

(GF, NF)

MULTIPURPOSE CRUMBLE TOPPING

Use this to sprinkle on top of muffins, loaves, cakes and pies. This recipe makes enough to sprinkle on a loaf or a batch of muffins, but feel free to double it if you like lots of crumble to top your pie.

MAKES about 1 cup (250 mL)
COOK TIME 5 minutes
SPECIAL EQUIPMENT NEEDED box grater

½ cup (125 mL) all-purpose flour or Gluten-Free All-Purpose Flour (see p. 24)

3 Tbsp (45 mL) rolled oats

1 tsp (5 mL) groud cinnamon

Pinch of salt

2 Tbsp (30 mL) sugar

1 Tbsp (15 mL) honey or maple syrup

3 Tbsp (45 mL) cold butter, grated

3 Tbsp (45 mL) hemp seeds (optional)

1. In a bowl, stir together the flour, oats, cinnamon, salt and sugar. Drizzle honey or maple syrup overtop.
2. Grate butter overtop and, using your hands, blend mixture until crumbly.
3. Stir in hemp seeds, if using, and sprinkle on top of anything you are baking that needs a crumbly topping.
4. Best kept in the fridge until needed. Freezer friendly.

CRUMBLE TIP

- Don't want to get your hands dirty? Put all ingredients in a food processor and pulse until you have a crumbly topping.

(V, GF, NF)

ICE CREAM–TRUCK CHOCOLATE CRACKLE (FOR COLD TREATS)

This is that magical chocolate shell coating you thought you could only get from an ice cream truck. Who knew how easy it is to make at home? You are only two ingredients away from drizzling chocolate crackle over a big bowl of vanilla ice cream.

MAKES 1 cup (250 mL)
TOTAL TIME 5 minutes

⅓ cup (80 mL) coconut oil (expeller-pressed if you want less coconut flavour)

¾ cup (185 mL) chocolate chips or chopped chocolate (65% or higher)

1. Melt coconut oil with chocolate in a small pot over medium-low heat.
2. Let cool and store in a jar with a lid, or in a sealed container at room temperature. Drizzle overtop of ice cream, or anything ice cold for that matter. As soon as it hits the cold it will freeze to form that childhood crackle topping we adore.
3. Give it a good stir before using. This will keep for at least a month, however mine has never lasted more than a few days.

CRACKLE TIP

- If the mixture solidifies, heat the container in a hot water bath.

MERINGUES AND AN ETON MESS

Meringues—aka the solution to your egg white problem. Whenever I make vanilla pudding (see p. 170), pound cake or anything with a lot of egg yolks, I'm left with a load of egg whites. I don't like to waste anything in my kitchen, so instead of throwing them out I save the whites and make meringues!

These sweet pillowy clouds are easy to make and a huge hit at my house. Serve them on their own or as an Eton Mess, meaning broken up with a big dollop of whipped cream and seasonal berries. This traditional English dessert was served at Eton College in their tuck shop, dating back to the 1930s. Here you go, a 2-in-1 dessert that everyone loves, any night of the week. It just goes to show that sometimes simple simply is the best!

(GF, NF)

MERINGUES

MAKES eight to twelve 3-inch (8 cm) nests
PREP TIME 10 minutes
BAKE TIME 2 hours
SPECIAL EQUIPMENT NEEDED stand mixer with a whisk attachment or handheld mixer

3 egg whites

1 tsp (5 mL) lemon juice

¾ cup (185 mL) superfine or caster sugar

1 tsp (5 mL) Pure Vanilla Extract (see p. 14)

1. Preheat oven to 200°F (95°C) and line a baking sheet.
2. In a clean bowl, beat egg whites with a whisk attachment until peaks form and they have doubled in volume, about 3–5 minutes.
3. While beating, add lemon juice and slowly pour in the sugar 1 Tbsp (15 mL) at a time until all of it is incorporated. Continue to beat until whites are stiff and glossy. Beat in vanilla.
4. Using a piping bag or spoon, make mounds or nests about 3 inches (8 cm) in diameter on the baking sheet.
5. Bake 1½–2 hours in the oven until the meringues are crisp and lift easily off the sheet. They should sound hollow when tapped underneath.
6. Let cool completely on a wire rack before storing in an airtight container for up to 2 days.

MERINGUE TIPS

- You need a clean dry bowl (preferably not plastic) when dealing with whipped egg whites. Meringues do not like moisture or any traces of fat or grease. It is also not ideal to bake them on a hot humid day.
- The finer the granules of sugar, the more easily they dissolve into the egg whites, giving the meringues a smoother consistency. However, when I was growing up my mom always used regular granulated sugar and her meringues always turned out just fine. So, don't worry if you don't have superfine sugar, just use what you have.
- Make sure to add the sugar slowly so that it's fully incorporated into the egg whites. If there are still granular bits at the bottom you will end up with those weird weepy meringues that look like they're sweating. There is nothing wrong with that, but if you want to avoid it just add the sugar slowly, bit by bit.

COOL FACT: MORE THINGS YOU MAY WANT TO KNOW ABOUT EGGS

Cold eggs are easier to separate than room-temperature eggs. However, room-temperature whites whisk better, and you get more height from them. If you have the time, separate eggs right out of the fridge, but let the whites come to room temperature for 30 minutes before beating.

(GF, NF)

ETON MESS

MAKES 4 servings
TOTAL TIME 10 minutes

2 cups (500 mL) seasonal fruit of choice (approx.), cut into bite-sized pieces

2 Tbsp (30 mL) sugar, maple syrup or honey

2 cups (500 mL) whipping cream (35%)

½ tsp (2 mL) ground cinnamon

4–6 meringue nests

1. Macerate or toss fruit with the sugar, maple syrup or honey and let stand for at least 10 minutes, or until you have a sugary syrup.
2. Whip cream with the cinnamon until you have soft billowy peaks.
3. Break up meringues and serve layered, or as messy as you like, in a bowl with the macerated fruit and whipped cream.

SAVED MY LIFE: MEASURING TAPE AND OFFICE SUPPLIES
Draw circles on parchment with a pencil as a guide when piping nests. I have a measuring tape, Sharpies, a pencil, labels, Post-it notes and binder clips all in one of my kitchen drawers.

(V, GF, LS)

NO-CHEESE CHERRY CHEESECAKE

I saved the best for last. This is that little sliver of something you need to finish a meal perfectly. Also, everything in it is actually good for you! It is decadent without being heavy and easy to make, since there is nothing to cook or bake. Perfect for a hot summer's day.

You throw around the terms raw and vegan when talking about a dessert and some people may groan. So just think of this as a cheese-less cheesecake. Or sell it to your guests as the "ultimate cherry cream pie." The combination of puréed cashews, fresh lemon juice and coconut oil will give you that same luscious cream cheese cheesecake consistency. Very nutrient dense, so a little of this goes a long way.

Another one of the many reasons why I love this recipe is that it can also be served right out of the freezer on a hot day, like a layered ice cream cake.

SOAK TIME 2 hours
PREP TIME 30 minutes
SET TIME 2 hours
SPECIAL EQUIPMENT NEEDED springform pan, food processor and/or a good blender

CRUST

1 cup (250 mL) walnuts, almonds or hazelnuts

¼ cup (60 mL) unsweetened flaked or shredded coconut

¼ cup (60 mL) hemp hearts (seeds)

Pinch of salt

½ cup (125 mL) packed pitted Medjool dates (about 6)

NO-CHEESE CHEESECAKE

3 cups (750 mL) cashews, soaked in water for 2 hours

½ cup (125 mL) fresh lemon juice

½ cup (125 mL) maple syrup

½ cup (125 mL) coconut oil, melted

1 vanilla bean, seeds only or 2 tsp (10 mL) Pure Vanilla Extract (see p. 14)

2 cups (500 mL) pitted cherries (if frozen, thaw)

1. Grease a springform pan with coconut oil and line with a parchment circle to fit the bottom.
2. In a food processor, pulse the walnuts, coconut, hemp hearts and salt until coarsely ground. Add in dates and continue to pulse 1–2 minutes, or until you have a wet sandy mixture that sticks together when pressed with fingers. Transfer crust mixture to the bottom of the pan and with fingers or the back of a spoon press to make into a single, even layer.
3. To make the cheesecake, drain and rinse soaked cashews. Add cashews and all other ingredients except the cherries into a blender or food processor. Blend until smooth.
4. Pour two-thirds of this mixture onto the crust and level with a small offset spatula or the back of spoon.
5. Add cherries to the leftover cashew mixture and blend until smooth. Pour onto cheesecake and level to make an even layer.
6. Cover cake with plastic wrap and freeze for at least 2 hours. Remove cake from springform pan sides when frozen. Let sit it the fridge to thaw for at least 30 minutes before serving. Can also be served frozen.

NO-CHEESE CHEESECAKE TIPS

- No cherries? Just substitute with 2 cups (500 mL) of any other fruit that's in season.
- If you want to get fancy, like in this photo, take a third of the vanilla-cashew mixture and reserve, then blend the remainder with the cherries. Reserve ½ cup (125 mL) of this cherry mixture for decoration and use the rest as your bottom cherry layer. Freeze until set, about an hour. Carefully pour and level the vanilla-cashew layer next. Pipe dots of the cherry mixture on top and swirl with a toothpick to your liking.

PICNIC
SIDE
HAM
FIGURE 2 : PORK

ACKNOWLEDGEMENTS

Honestly, writing this cookbook was not easy. It was, for sure, a labour of love, and it would not have been possible without the help of a whole bunch of pretty amazing people. As with the harder things in life, a whole lot of good things came out of the process.

First off, I need to thank my children, for continuing to be my harshest food critics and putting up with some of the crazy things I have made them eat over the years. I only hope that all the cooking you see me do will pleasantly ingrain itself in a small part of your memory.

I am so very grateful for my family and friends, you know who you are . . . the ones who saw me through some of my "not so good" moments, never judged and still treated me with dignity and respect.

I am no writer, so to the people at Whitecap and Westwood Creative Artists I thank you for believing in me and allowing me the freedom to find my voice.

There were many generous, creative and passionate people that were a huge support in the creation of this cookbook. I thank you all for your precious time and patience. A few key players in the logistical execution of this book were Michelle Bish, who kept me on track when life got in the way; Reena Newman, for all her pretty pictures and helping me breeze through the process; and Lauran Branson for her abundance of colour-coordinated props and an "eye" like no other. Zoe Kazokas helped me in the beginning when I was juggling recipe testing with recipe writing. Dana Harrison assisted in keeping the creative thoughts churning and keeping us on track within our small but super-efficient photography team. Thanks to Sage Dakota for having my back and reminding me why I started doing all this.

Being a person managing anxiety and depression, I want to acknowledge all my fellow comrades living with mental illness. It is no easy feat, even on the best of days. Slow and steady, tiny steps and don't ever give up.

INDEX